Mike,

 Your system knowledge, customer relations and responsiveness have been a key factor in our continued success. Thanks for your many years of loyal support.

D. [signature] 12/90

35508
$ 22⁰⁰

NW History
WA / Kent

P9-BYD-818

KENT

Pictorial Research by Linda Van Nest

"Partners in Progress" by Lynn Johnson

Produced in cooperation with
the Kent Chamber of Commerce

Windsor Publications, Inc.
Chatsworth, California

KENT
VALLEY OF OPPORTUNITY

AN ILLUSTRATED HISTORY
BY FLORENCE K. LENTZ

Windsor Publications, Inc.—History Book Division
Managing Editor: Karen Story
Design Director: Alexander D'Anca
Photo Director: Susan L. Wells
Executive Editor: Pamela Schroeder

Staff for *Kent: Valley of Opportunity*
Senior Manuscript Editor: Jerry Mosher
Photo Editor: Patty Salkeld
Editor, Corporate Biographies: Melissa W. Patton
Production Editor, Corporate Biographies: Justin Scupine
Customer Service Manager: Phyllis Feldman-Schroeder
Editorial Assistants: Elizabeth Anderson, Dominique Jones, Kim Kievman, Michael Nugwynne,
Kathy B. Peyser, Theresa J. Solis
Publisher's Representative, Corporate Biographies: David Cook, Elizabeth Cook
Designer: Ellen Ifrah
Layout Artists, Corporate Biographies: Bonnie Felt, Tanya Maiboroda
Layout Artist: Editorial: Michael Burg

Windsor Publications, Inc.
Elliot Martin, Chairman of the Board
James L. Fish III, Chief Operating Officer
Michele Sylvestro, Vice President/Sales-Marketing
Mac Buhler, Vice President/Sponsor Acquisitions

©1990 Windsor Publications, Inc.
All rights reserved
Published 1990
Printed in the United States of America
First Edition

Library of Congress Cataloging-in-Publication Data

Lentz, Florence K.

Kent—valley of opportunity : an illustrated history / by Florence K. Lentz ; pictorial research by
Linda Van Nest ; "Partners in progress" by Lynn Johnson. —1st ed.

p. 128 cm. 22 x 28

"Produced in cooperation with the Kent Chamber of Commerce."

Includes bibliographic references (p. 123) and index.

ISBN 0-89781-356-1

1. Kent (Wash.)—History. 2. Kent Region (Wash.)—History. 3. Kent (Wash.)—Description—Views.
4. Kent Region Wash.)—Description and travel—Views. 5. Kent (Wash.)—Industries.
6. Kent Region (Wash.)—Industries. I. Kent Chamber of Commerce. II. Title.
F899.K36L46   1990   90-38925
979.777—dc20   CIP

*FRONTISPIECE: Calm, serene, and alive with 47 acres of flora
and fauna, Lake Fenwick Park offers year-round fishing and miles
of hiking trails that meander through the park and around the lake.
A recent upgrade of the park included the installment of a bridge
to Lake Island, a floating dock. Photo by Gary Greene*

Contents

Foreword

In 1968, I stood on a street corner in California, wishing that I could leave suburbia behind and live in a small community again as I had when I was growing up. I got my wish, and that year Boeing paid for our move to Kent.

We rented Tom O'Connell's farmhouse across the Green River from the Boeing Space Center. The O'Connells' dairy farm had provided milk for the community since the turn of the century, until state laws prohibited the retail sale of raw milk. The O'Connells have returned to the farm, but horse breeding is now the family business.

Each morning at 6 a.m., when the white owl would swoop past my kitchen window and into the barn to take his place in the rafters, I was glad all over again that we had made the move.

The first time I shopped in downtown Kent, I walked into the dime store with my two little boys, four and five years old, in tow.

After selecting our purchases, we took our place in the line at the cash register right behind an elderly woman who was leaning on a cane. As she began to open her coin purse to pay, the hinge of her purse gave way and quarters, dimes, nickels, and pennies rolled out onto the floor.

I was conditioned by recent experience in crowded stores and automatically stepped around her to lay my purchases on the counter, expecting the sales clerk would want to keep the line moving and let the woman find her own change.

To my surprise, the clerk closed the cash register, stepped around the counter and stooped to pick up the change that had rolled in her direction. Everything came to a halt as others stooped to help, while I stood there rather sheepishly watching my sons gleefully join in the game of pick-up. With the coins retrieved, the woman completed her purchase and moved away with a cheery thank you to all.

The warmth and congeniality in that store was so welcoming. I knew this was my kind of community. Caring people took the time to help!

Kent was still a farming community then. Rhubarb fields stretched from the corner of 212th South along the Valley Highway, and cabbages littered the side of the road after rolling off trucks headed for the cannery. Seattle radio disc jockeys discussed when Mr. Okimoto's sweet and wonderful corn would be ripe, and you could buy Swedish or purple potatoes from a farmer's barn. Southcenter was just fallow fields near a big highway interchange.

Since that time, valley fields have given way to warehouses, and apartment buildings have sprung up overnight. Change continues to be a way of life. This history depicts the caring people who shaped the change.

Kent people with the vision to work for a good library and for a versatile senior center, for parks, for an energetic arts commission, for building new schools and passing school levies and more, continue to demonstrate the quality and extent of the caring.

The Kent Chamber of Commerce has been an active voice in the community. This book was made possible by the interest of chamber volunteers and sponsoring corporations.

The publication is divided into two sections—a history of the social and cultural life of Kent, followed by a look at Kent's economic history through brief vignettes of sponsoring corporations. The intent is to capture the major events, the actors, themes, trends, and turning points of our past.

The book contains stories of some of Kent's people and some of their accomplishments, but it is only the beginning of a full involvement with the community. My dream is that this history will spark your interest, and you will want to get involved, learn more, and launch activities that document Kent's story. Working in concert with groups such as the King County Landmarks Commission, Kent's social studies teachers, the White River Valley Historical Society, and the Kent Chamber of Commerce Foundation for Arts and Education, we, as a community, can commemorate our past.

Laurel Whitehurst
Member, King County Landmarks Commission; Chair, Kent Library Board; first Director of the Kent Saturday Market; past Member of the Kent Chamber of Commerce Board of Directors; Public Relations Consultant

Acknowledgments

The moment I began, I knew that I would not be "writing" the history of Kent so much as assembling it, piece by piece, with the help of those who have lived it and recorded it before me. Wherever I turned in my research, I found an abundance of useful material. The limits of space and time prevent including every interesting aspect of Kent's past. The result, instead, is an overview that weaves together the writings and recollections of many sources.

First thanks belong to the quintessential historian of King County, Clarence Bagley, whose comprehensive volumes of the 1920s never fail to elicit new bits of information at each reading. For a running, on-the-scene account chock full of local color, no source has been more basic and more valuable than that venerable local newspaper, the *Valley Daily News*. To others who have recorded the story of Kent and its valley setting—C. E. Cameron, Stan Flewelling, Charles Payton, and Linda Van Nest—I extend my thanks for paving the way.

It was the people of Kent who breathed life into my framework of dates and themes. Tremendous thanks must go to Rae Reitan, City Historian, a veritable fount of wisdom on Kent history. With her late husband, Ed Reitan, Rae collected the memories and memorabilia of Kent for forty-some years, and these she shared with me in a most generous and entertaining way. There are many whom I did not meet face-to-face whose personal reminiscences appear in this book through the courtesy of the oral history project "Kent 1910-1960," conducted by the Green River Community College History Department. Thanks are due to Steve Carkeek at the College Instructional Media Center for making three hours of project tapes available.

Many others willingly related the experiences of their own lives and careers in Kent. Particularly generous with their time and insight were: Tom Bailey, former City Councilman and Chamber of Commerce secretary; Hardy Drangsholt, arts and library activist; James Harris, Director, Kent Planning Department; Jerry McCaughan, Property Manager, Kent Engineering Department; Laurel Whitehurst, arts, preservation, and education activist; Barney Wilson, Director, Kent Parks and Recreation Department; and Judy Woods, City Councilwoman and History Department Chair, Green River Community College.

To all those who responded to my inquiries by offering facts, printed materials, or access to their files I am grateful: Virginia Cross, Pat Curran, Sylvia Gray, Phil Jeter, Marie Jensen, Judy Parker, Patrice Thorell, Helen Wickstrom, and Nancy Woo.

The best of support and encouragement came from Barbara Simpson and the Kent Chamber of Commerce, from Joe Koch and others at the White River Valley Historical Society, from Deb Barker, my research assistant, and from Kathy Lynn, my speedy typist and friend.

Last but certainly not least, a special thank you goes to Gary, Laura, and Cap, who patiently endured many late suppers and lost evenings and weekends.

Florence K. Lentz

While accompanying Captain George Vancouver on his voyages to the northern Pacific Ocean in 1792, John Sykes drew this imposing view of Mount Rainier from Admiralty Inlet on south Puget Sound. The pole is one-half of a Native American trap; when strung with a net, it ensnared ducks purposely frightened by the hunters. Courtesy, Special Collections Division, University of Washington Libraries

CHAPTER ONE

The Lure of White River

In the broad river valley where the city of Kent now stands, salt water tides once ebbed and flowed at the base of East Hill. Whales cavorted in the icy blue waters and gulls circled high above an ancient hook-shaped arm of Puget Sound. Then one fabled day, over 5,000 years ago, a geological disaster of epic proportions set in motion the eventual extinction of that branch of the sea and gave birth to the fertile White River Valley. To understand the ceaseless evolution of the age-old valley and its river system is to understand in large part the history of the community of Kent.

Primitive people digging shellfish along the beach may well have witnessed that long-ago cataclysm. Native mythology alludes to a time when the shimmering summit cone of Mount Rainier collapsed and spewed forth a deadly avalanche of mud and rock. A steaming mass surged down the north face of the mountain, obliterating all life in its path. On the Enumclaw Plateau, 20 miles southeast of Kent, modern-day archaeologists recently found evidence of human encampments buried under 75 feet of mud. The Osceola Mudflow, as geologists have since termed it, emptied its load of debris into the salt water bay at the present site of Auburn.

In the aftermath, the White River cut a new channel from its glacial source on Mount Rainier deep into the surface of the mudflow's lobe. Most significantly, the lower course of the river was deflected to the north. Its waters sluiced down heavy deposits of coarse gravel and fine sediment from the mudflow and created an ever-extending alluvial fan. Over time, the alluvium built up above sea level and the White River Valley emerged from the sea.

By the beginning of the nineteenth century, the valley cradled a complex but well-established river system. Still, it was much different in its configuration than it is today. In those days, White River was the dominant stream and gave the valley its name. Just north of Auburn, the Green River emptied into the White and was considered tributary to it. The enlarged channel meandered many times back and forth across the wide, flat valley floor. North of the present city of Kent, at Tukwila, White River merged with the murky waters of the Black, an outlet of Lake Washington. Together they flowed through a narrow canyon as the deep Duwamish River, and emptied through shifting channels across a vast delta, into Elliott Bay on Puget Sound.

For centuries, mountain snowmelts in the spring and heavy rains in the fall subjected the lower valley to semi-annual flooding. Each time the river overflowed its banks, it blanketed the valley floor with a layer of rich alluvium. On the poorly drained floodplain an extensive network of wetlands evolved. The river and its marshes, swamps, and woodlands hosted an abundance of life, both terrestrial and aquatic.

Nourished by loamy soil and copious rains, vegetation grew thick on the valley floor. Cottonwood, ash, bigleaf maple, and alder trees were mixed with stands of fir and cedar. The underbrush was a tangle of vine maple, Oregon grape, salal, and salmonberries. Here and there were small open meadows thick with grasses.

Small mammals such as river otters, muskrat, longtailed weasel, beavers, and cottontails made the river corridor their home, as did the red fox, coyote, and striped skunk. Vast flocks of migrating birds shadowed the river valley for days on end, and some species of waterfowl wintered there. Wild ducks and Canada geese, coots and mergansers, blue heron and bald eagles were regular visitors. Grouse, pheasant, and quail flourished.

The river itself gave life to an endless variety of fish. Salmon species included the chinook, coho, chum, pink, and sockeye. From the sea to spawning grounds deep in the foothills of the Cascades, the river served as their watery conduit.

The abundance of the river valley sustained a native people whose nomadic existence was ordered by the seasons. We know little of their ancient civilization prior to the onset of recorded history in the region. What is known with greatest certainty today about the valley's native culture dates from after the time of Captain George Vancouver's voyage of discovery on Puget Sound in 1792.

The people of the valley were loosely organized in independent family groups who wintered together at numerous permanent village sites along the rivers and streams of the drainage system. Marriage outside the family group broadened each village's economic and social relationships by extending their rights to food-gathering at more distant locations. With direct access to the high mountain passes, natives of the White and Green rivers established especially strong kinship, language, and trade ties with the Yakima and Klickitat peoples east of the Cascade Mountains.

In the mid-1850s, in preparation for treaty negotiations, the territorial government of Washington sought to classify bands of Indians living along each drainage system. Ethnographer George Gibbs, working for Territorial Governor Isaac Stevens, conducted the first "census" of native peoples in 1854. Among other tribes whose designated spokesman was Chief Seattle, Gibbs identified

three groups on the White and Green river drainage: the Stkamish on the lower White through what is now the city of Kent, the Smulkamish on the upper White, and the Skopamish on the upper Green.

The Stkamish, Smulkamish, and Skopamish peoples were the ancestors of the present-day Muckleshoot tribe. Before the creation of a tribal reservation in 1857, however, the name Muckleshoot was not applied to these people, nor were they a single tribe as such. Instead, they referred to themselves broadly in relation to their habitat; thus, as "river" or "mountain" people, they were distinguished from "saltwater" people. Further, each band was identified by the name of its village plus the suffix "absh," meaning "people of."

There were several native villages along the banks of White River in the area now included within Kent city limits. The northernmost site was Stek or Stokk, meaning "log jam," a place where canoes required portage, later known by the pioneers as Van Doren's Landing. A short distance upriver was the village of Teutap-alt or "Flea's House." In native mythology, Elk's daughter came to this place and was married to Flea. Still farther upstream where the 78th Street railroad bridge crosses the river at Thomas was Pob-sholku. Five miles farther south at the confluence of the White and Green rivers was the large and important vil-

lage of Ilalqo, meaning "striped water."

In each village, the people built sturdy cedar longhouses on shelves of well-drained ground. Rectangular in plan and 40 to 100 feet in length, these large cedar log superstructures supported exterior planking. Most villages consisted of two or three houses, but Ilalqo boasted 17. Each house was designed to hold multiple families, generally from four to six. Inside, the walls were lined with cattail mats for insulation. Sleeping berths, which doubled as bench seating during the day, surrounded the perimeter. Firewood, dried foods and roots, basketry, and tools were all stored inside.

When the salmonberry sprouts appeared and the spring winds began to blow, families embarked upon their seasonal wanderings to traditional fishing, hunting, and berrying grounds. People carried their prized cattail mats along and these were draped and fastened over poles, forming temporary summer shelters. Women trav-

eled west to the Sound to clam-digging beaches at Three Tree Point and what is now Saltwater State Park. The clams were said to be at their best when the dogwood was in full bloom. For winter food and trade with tribes east of the mountains, smoked clams were a highly prized delicacy. Spring root-gathering on the open prairies was followed by berry picking in foothills and lowland bogs. Elderberries, cranberries, gooseberries, wild straw-

LEFT: The construction of a salmon weir in the White River near the Muckleshoot Reservation is depicted here around 1903. The weir was used to block the passage of fish during the salmon runs, allowing men using dip nets to catch the fish while standing on the weir platform. Courtesy, White River Valley Historical Museum

FACING PAGE: The longhouse, built by the native peoples in each village, had a fire pit in the center with fish drying overhead and sleeping platforms around the perimeter. The interior of this Chinook lodge is similar to those found throughout the Puget Sound region. This image was sketched by A.T. Agate of the Wilkes expedition in 1841. Courtesy, Special Collections Division, University of Washington Libraries

BELOW: Native peoples erected temporary summer camps of poles and cattail mats during fishing season or when gathering food. This 1912 photo depicts a camp on Puget Sound with a small dugout canoe used for fishing. Courtesy, Special Collections Division, University of Washington Libraries, Edward Curtis

berries, thimbleberries, and blackberries grew in profusion. The huckleberry harvest in the mountains was an eagerly anticipated social event lasting several weeks.

While women gathered and processed roots and berries, men hunted elk and deer, bear and mountain goat, and some species of small game. Simple spears and ingenious aerial nets were used to capture grouse, pheasant, and duck.

But for Muckleshoot men, the year's most important work took place on the rivers. Indian fisheries extended from the upper reaches of tributary streams to the waters of the Sound. From May to November, the river witnessed runs of salmon so abundant it was said that on small streams one could literally walk across their backs. Fish weirs and basket traps were the favored means of harvesting large quantities of fish when the runs were at their peak. Late into the night, by the light of the moon or torch, skilled fishermen crouched on platforms above the water's surface armed with dip nets. Large catches were dried for fall consumption or smoked as a winter food source.

The valley's extended river network not only met most of the natives' subsistence needs, it also served as a corridor of transportation. There was no need to contemplate carving roads through the tangled underbrush as long as shallow shovel-nosed cedar canoes skimmed so swiftly and efficiently over riffles and sunken logs. The river was a natural highway, providing easy access to the saltwater Sound, to the inland bodies of Lake Washington and Lake Sammamish, and deep into the mountains up the interconnected channels of the White, the Green, the Black, and the Cedar.

ABOVE: Constructed in 1833 and depicted here in the 1880s, the blockhouse at Fort Nisqually for many decades served as the main trading post for the trappers and settlers of the south Puget Sound region. Courtesy, Special Collections Division, University of Washington Libraries

FACING PAGE: David and Irena Neely, originally from Tennessee, settled near present-day Kent in 1854 on a Donation Land Claim along the White River. Their farming was interrupted by the conflict between the Native Americans and settlers in 1855 when Neely served as a lieutenant in the Territorial Army. In later years the Neely farm became the first post office in the area, with David Neely as postmaster. Courtesy, Judy Neely Roush Collection

The first extended contact with Europeans that White and Green river natives experienced was undoubtedly through trade with the powerful Hudson's Bay Company. From 1818 to 1846, Britain and the United States jointly controlled the vast Oregon Country, but it was the British Hudson's Bay Company, headquartered for most of that period at Fort Vancouver on the Columbia, that brought stability and government to the region. People of the White River drainage enjoyed easy water access to the nearest trading post at Fort Nisqually on southern Puget Sound, established in 1833 near the present-day town of Steilacoom. There, firearms, blankets, tools, and trinkets were exchanged for beaver, otter, and muskrat pelts.

of unrivalled fertility." Ebey followed the Black River branch of the "Dewams" east into Lake Washington, but did not omit a mention of the White River country:

Of the left bank of the Dewams little is known, until you get into the region of country where the wagon road crosses the same. The Indians represent the character of the country above much the same as that already described. Where the wagon road crosses the river, plains of unrivalled fertility are found, covered with the most luxurious growth of grass I have ever met with . . .

Fertile bottomland and open prairies were exactly the sort of land most desired by westering settlers. In 1850, the U.S. government made migration to the Oregon Territory more attractive than ever with passage of the Donation Land Act. This legislation offered free land to white settlers who would occupy and improve a claim for five years. Single men were allotted 320 acres, and married couples 640 acres. This inducement, coupled with the stabilizing effect of the British-American boundary treaty in 1846 and the establishment of a territorial government in 1848, triggered the first wave of settlement in the White River Valley.

In September 1851, when Henry Van Asselt, Luther Collins, and Jacob and Samuel Maple selected claims on the lower Duwamish near the area now known as Georgetown, they became the first permanent settlers in King County. From Alki

For their own part, Hudson's Bay employees may have traveled the valley in the 1830s and 1840s in their exploratory voyages. In particular, one Jean Baptiste Ouvrie expressed an interest in the river and in the country around Elliott Bay, and to his superior, Dr. William Fraser Tolmie, chief factor at Fort Nisqually, he described it as "equal in size to the Cowlitz." Tolmie referred to "Ouvrie's River" in his journal account of an expedition to Alki Point. Isaac Ebey, a prominent American settler, made more detailed written observations of the valley in correspondence with Dr. Tolmie in 1850. With an eye toward the river's economic potential, Ebey noted the "deep channel and placid current" and described a "rich bottomland, not heavily timbered, with here and there a beautiful plain

Point near the mouth of the Duwamish, David Denny penned a letter that same autumn to his brother Arthur, whose efforts would soon lead to the founding of Seattle. "Come as soon as you can," David wrote, "we have found a valley that will accommodate one thousand families." By 1853, when a rude wagon road over Naches Pass was pushed through the Cascades, pioneers A.L. Porter, Dominick Corcoran, and James Riley descended into the upper river valley over Indian trails and settled on the Enumclaw Plateau.

In the heart of the White River country, within the modern-day city limits of Kent, new arrivals staked their claims in quick succession: Henry Adams, Samuel Russell, Moses Kirkland, Robert Beaty, David and Irena Neely, Enos Cooper, and

Major General Isaac I. Stevens served as the first territorial governor of Washington Territory from 1853 to 1857. After dealing with the Indian Wars in Washington Territory, Stevens later volunteered for service in the Civil War and was killed at the Battle of Chantilly in 1862. Courtesy, Special Collections Division, University of Washington Libraries

John and Nancy Thomas. Donation Land Claim records kept by the General Land Office from 1853 to 1855 indicate that in all of King County the most desirable place to settle was along the banks of the White River.

The pioneers set to work immediately clearing the land in preparation for crops. They removed stands of trees, grubbed out stumps, and planted basic subsistence crops. Before the winter rains they built simple cabins of logs with cedar shake roofing and river rock chimneys. Crude roads of puncheon were laid over marshy areas where necessary, but the major highway of transportation in those first hard years was the river.

In the earliest years of white settlement in the valley, relations remained friendly with the native population. The pioneers availed themselves of Indian assistance in clearing the land, transporting goods along the river, and supplementing their first meager harvests. For their part, the natives were not opposed to a measured white presence among them, as it had up to then enhanced their trade opportunities and relative strength among other tribes. But as non-natives arrived in increasing numbers, basic cultural conflicts over the use of the land emerged. By coveting the rich bottomlands and open prairies for farms, the settlers unknowingly disturbed Indian "gardens," the meadows kept artificially open by periodic burnings to enhance the growth of certain berries and roots. On riverbanks, the new homesteads often encompassed or butted up to ancient native villages, traditional fishing and plant gathering sites, or sacred land forms and assembly places. As the native peoples witnessed their diminishing access to the life-giving river corridor and realized no compensation for it, their anxiety grew.

By the fall of 1854, settlers and natives alike sensed the mounting tension. White and Green river bands were contacted by their Yakima and Klickitat kin from east of the mountains. Loyalties were tested and alliances strengthened.

In an attempt to diffuse the volatile situation, the newly appointed governor of Washington Terri-

Emily I. Denny's painting of the Battle of Seattle on January 26, 1856, shows settlers scrambling for the blockhouse while the sloop of war, USS Decatur, stands offshore. White River settlers, such as the Neely and Russell families, fled to Seattle during this period of hostilities. Courtesy, Museum of History and Industry, Seattle, Washington

tory, Isaac Stevens, initiated an aggressive drive to extinguish native title to the land through treaty negotiations. But the treaties only increased the growing distrust and resentment on the part of the natives. On January 25, 1855, Chief Seattle, a headman of the Suquamish tribe across the Sound, signed away the native claim to the entire Duwamish-White-Green River drainage system in exchange for a promise of reservation lands on the Kitsap Peninsula. His Duwamish kin, and bands of the upper White and Green rivers whom Seattle supposedly represented, could not accept the terms of this agreement. The Point Elliott Treaty went unratified over the course of the year, and in the meantime, settlers continued to arrive and take up claims at White River.

The Yakima War erupted in the late summer of 1855 across the whole of Washington Territory. On the west side of the mountains, conflict was centered in the upper White River Valley of King County. In October, several pioneer families in the vicinity of Auburn were attacked. The "White River Massacre" sent shock waves throughout the Puget Sound region. Panicked King County settlers fled to Seattle where they wintered in the safety of the Fort Decatur blockhouse, but most able-bodied men joined the Washington Territory Volunteers and spent the winter marching and fighting in the chilly rain.

On January 26, 1856, a force of Yakima, Klickitat, Nisqually, Skopamish, and Smulkamish attacked the village of Seattle. The cannons of the warship *Decatur,* anchored in Elliott Bay, are credited with preventing the destruction of the town. The Battle of Seattle was the last organized offensive of the native forces. Although there were brave skirmishes here and there on into the spring, the sheer number and superior weaponry of white forces soon prevailed.

The Indian Wars in King County were a sad and desolate chapter in the valley's history. Over 60 men, women, and children both native and white had lost their lives, and that amounted to almost 10 percent of the population. Fine leaders had been sacrificed on either side. The country lay devastated, farms and ancient native villages leveled by fire. Half of the White River settlers who had fled to Seattle sold their claims, never to return to rebuild; others delayed one or two years before venturing back.

Some native people of the lower valley were assigned to the Suquamish Reservation at Port Madison. In response to persistent objections from upper river tribes, the Muckleshoot Reservation was created by Executive Order on January 20, 1857. The name of the reservation, later applied to all of the people living there, was simply taken from the name of the prairie upon which it was located, southeast of Auburn. Native villages in the vicinity of the present-day city of Kent were extinguished forever, and the people were sentenced to reservations or left to fend for themselves with their landless kin on the lower Duwamish River.

Captain James J. Crow and Emma Russell Crow posed for a family portrait with all 13 of their children, in-laws, and grandchildren. Captain Crow purchased and planted some of the first hop roots in the White River Valley. With dollars from hop sales he purchased the sternwheeler Lily *and built a three-story mansion. Courtesy, White River Valley Historical Museum*

The Fertile Valley

In his classic account of the old Northwest, *Pioneer Days on Puget Sound,* Seattle founder Arthur A. Denny recalled that the decade following the Indian War was a time of "pinching want and great privation" for the settlers of King County. Pioneer businesses, road building, and improvements to the land came to a virtual standstill. Emigrants and natives alike lived in fear of hostile reprisals. Word of the violence spread eastward, and no new settlers were drawn to the White River Valley. To provide vegetables and grain for the hardy souls who remained, farmers cultivated crops in the lower Duwamish valley under armed guard.

During this lull in settlement, developments elsewhere set the stage for a new wave of immigration in the 1860s and 1870s. The accessibility of the Puget Sound country improved with the construction of a railroad across the Isthmus of Panama in 1855. Expanding maritime traffic on the Sound, and the completion of the Military Road from Fort Steilacoom to Seattle in 1860, made travel to Elliott Bay and the White River Valley easier. Veterans of the Fraser River gold rush in British Columbia made their way down the Sound in search of fertile farmland in the late 1850s, and the Homestead Act of 1863 encouraged further settlement.

A handful of the most determined pioneers returned to their White River claims in the late 1850s, among them the David A. Neely and the Samuel Russell families. The first of a new wave of emigrants, future builders of the community of Kent, arrived in 1859 when Thomas Moody Alvord bought out the fire-ravaged claim of Moses Kirkland for $300. Thomas Alvord and his wife, Maria Julia, were a resourceful and energetic pair, successful together as farmers, merchants, and traders. The Alvord family's busy river trade, prosperous ranch, and active role in community affairs spanned 50 years of pioneer life on White River.

In the 1860s came more newcomers who put down roots in the central valley and made their mark on the early history of Kent. Patrick Hayes arrived in 1860 and labored to build up a model hop and dairy farm. Prominent in the valley's Catholic community, Hayes later donated land for the Briscoe School. Richard Jeffs took up a claim in 1861. Together with his Native American wife, they developed a showplace farm and upon their deaths provided for the valley's first orphanage. Pioneer farmer and merchant John Langston came in 1862 and opened up a general merchandise store, said to have been the second in King County outside Seattle. From that busy location on the river, he operated an important ferry crossing and landing for some 15 years. Stephen Willis homesteaded a tract near the future townsite of Kent in 1865, and later gave his name to one of its major streets.

White River's most colorful pioneer family in the vicinity of Kent must have been that of James Jeremiah Crow. Hop farmer, riverboat captain, prospector, mayor, and real estate man, James J. Crow led a life as big as the country around him. In 1862 he eloped in a canoe up the White River with his bride, Emma Russell. Together they raised a family of 13 children, and eventually retired in Kent in a handsome residence that became a social center of the community.

In the early decades of valley settlement, before the platting and incorporation of Kent, farms and small settlements all along the river's meandering course, from its juncture with the Green to its confluence with the Black, were known collectively as White River. A post office of that name was established at David A. Neely's place in 1861. By 1870, White River had attained a population of 277, and all of the "good" well-drained bottomland had been claimed.

Farming and trade centers sprang up at various locations along the river at key crossroads

LEFT: Thomas M. Alvord was a successful early settler who farmed a large Donation Land Claim and also ran a river boat landing along the White River south of Kent. Native Americans supplied much of the farm labor during the growing season. Alvord is depicted here around the turn of the century with Preacher Bob, a Native American friend. Courtesy, White River Valley Historical Museum

FACING PAGE, TOP: Spearing salmon in the White River was not just an idle pastime for early settlers. The fall salmon runs brought hundreds of huge fish upriver to spawn. Smoked, dried, baked, or grilled, salmon provided both settlers and Native Americans with an important staple for their diets. Courtesy, White River Valley Historical Museum

FACING PAGE, BOTTOM: This 1907 view looks west along the main street of Orillia, north of Kent. Orillia was founded by Malcolm McDougall, a Canadian, who named the town after his hometown in Ontario. Courtesy, White River Valley Historical Museum

and river landings. One of the earliest was Maddocksville, situated on the west river bank across from Van Doren's ferry landing. Maddocksville is the only community on White River listed as such in *Choir's Pioneer Directory of The City of Seattle and King County in 1878.* Choir's proclaimed:

MADDOCKSVILLE . . . contains two churches, a schoolhouse and a store, and is just the place for families to settle who desire to cultivate a few acres, and enjoy the pure air and sweets of a country life . . . It was laid off and is owned by M. B. Maddocks, who offers it in small, choice lots, to actual setters, at remarkably cheap rates . . .

Another early settlement now within the city limits of Kent was Pialschie, located in the vicinity of Alvord's Landing, on land first occupied by the native village of Pob-sholku, and later claimed by John M. Thomas. Named for a well-known local Indian, "Pialschie" was later changed to "Thomas" when a post office was established there in 1906.

Just east of Maddocksville was O'Brien, a cluster of farms settled by a colony of Irish Catholics. First homesteaded by Terence O'Brien and his brother Morgan in 1868, the community grew in later years as a stop on the railroad.

The farmers of the White River Valley looked north to the milltown on Elliott Bay as an outlet for their produce. In those first hard years, settlers produced little extra beyond the subsistence needs of their own families. But it was not long before small quantities of White River potatoes, eggs, and butter found their way to markets in Seattle and San Francisco.

Potatoes were evidently the first crop raised in quantity for commercial purposes. When the newcomers arrived in Puget Sound country they found this staple under cultivation by native peoples who had been encouraged in this effort by Hudson's Bay Company practices. Another successful early cash crop was onions. Pioneer Patrick Hayes' first endeavor in the valley in 1861 was to raise two acres of onions on leased land. His bumper crop commanded such excellent prices that he was able to purchase his own tract of 150 acres. Thomas Alvord relied heavily on potatoes and onions during his earliest years on White River, but by 1868 he was also producing for commercial sale cabbage, peas, carrots, and turnips. Pears, plums, and apples were grown in the Alvord orchard, and by 1878, Moses Maddocks too was known for his prolific orchards.

As rapidly as their finances would allow, White River farmers acquired animal stock. Pork, beef, milk, butter, eggs, and wool garnered high prices on the Seattle market. Cattle, dairy cows, sheep, hogs, and chickens pastured on the undeveloped portions of a settler's claim brought a return on acreage not yet grubbed and plowed. Thomas Alvord actually made a profitable business of grazing and boarding cattle, oxen, and horses in the 1860s and 1870s. His Pialschie ranch served as a rest station for herds driven north to market from Oregon.

Grain and forage crops became an important aspect of valley agriculture in the 1860s and 1870s. Hay, timothy, oats, barley, and wheat accounted for much of a farmer's annual return. The damp climate presented some problems for the cultivation of wheat, but the demand for flour was great. Charles Ballard, son of a pioneer family from the south end of the valley, wrote of the challenge the wheat crop presented in those days:

Father tried raising wheat to make flour. The country had such early rains and so much moisture that it always grew so rank that it would fall down before it was ripe enough to be cut. Still he did so for several seasons, once taking out a load out to a grist mill on the Steilacoom plains. In later years there was a mill put in a little below the Stark place on the east side of White River (the Olson grist mill). The flour from this wheat made stick bread and as soon as we were able we bought our flour.

Year by year, as available acreage expanded through clearing of the land, as prices held firm and the rain and fertile soil brought repeated good harvests, and as transportation from farm to market improved, hard work paid off for the valley's pioneers. Thomas Alvord's log books reveal a healthy level of business activity among farmers of the central valley, in an economy based upon bartering of goods and labor, extension of credit, and a steady market demand. Labor was commonly supplied by local Indians who left the reservation for summer camps on the larger ranches during the growing season. For most settlers, native workers proved steady and reliable.

The magazine *West Shore, An Illustrated Journal of General Information Devoted to the Development of The Great West,* carried a feature article on the remarkable advancement of the White River Valley in October 1877:

ABOVE: *The Victorian-style Terence O'Brien house, with its gingerbread trim and double hung windows, is seen under construction in 1899. Lending his name to the town where he first homesteaded in 1868, O'Brien and his wife and sisters posed for a photo with the carpenters and bricklayers. Courtesy, White River Valley Historical Museum*

RIGHT: *Ezra Meeker of Puyallup, depicted here around 1920, was one of the larger "hop kings" of the south Puget Sound region. Meeker settled in Puyallup in 1862 and began raising hops in 1865. In 1878 James Crow and Richard Jeffs of Kent collected hop roots from Meeker's farm to begin cultivating the crop at their farms in the White River Valley. Courtesy, Seattle Post-Intelligencer Collection, Museum of History and Industry*

Twenty-two years finds the White River settlements extending up nearly to the mountains and through all tributary valleys. The forests are slowly giving way to farms. Fine meadows well set in the tame grasses, on which bands of choice dairy stock are thriving . . . Houses, farms and fences show a good degree of comfort and thrift on part of their owners, yet the depth and richness of the soil is the most marked feature . . . The river winds gracefully with gentle current, bending now to the range of hills to the right and now to those on the left, much like the beautiful rivers of New England. Autumn and winter storms of rain and snow often raise it quickly bank-ful and overflowing, and occasionally fill the valley . . . This process has gone on for ages until the whole valley . . . is formed into a continuous bed of choicest soil for the grasses, the cereals, the vegetables and the fruits . . . steamers run up the river from thirty to forty miles, bringing produce and lumber daily to the busy wharves at Seattle.

What the author of this appealing promotional piece failed to note was that an important new fac-

quantities of hops (one-half to one pound in size) for "household use," and had sold one ton of his crop in Seattle that very year.

Whatever their local origin, it is clear that hops had taken hold in White River by the late 1870s. A major turning point in the valley's history, the advent of hops would soon attract the first railroad, spur the founding of the town of Kent, and make overnight princes of many a poor valley farmer.

The earliest roads in King County were built through the White River Valley in the 1850s, the first by order of the Territorial Legislature to connect Seattle with the Fort Steilacoom-Fort Walla Walla wagon route across the Cascade mountains over Naches Pass. In 1860, the Military Road from Fort Steilacoom to Fort Bellingham was completed as far as Seattle by the U.S. Corps of Topographical Engineers along the hills west of present-day Kent. One pioneer later wrote:

Like the old Roman Roads of England this road paid but little attention to grades but went straight along the face of the hills until the summit was reached, so that it was necessary to double up the teams and pull one wagon up to the top and then go back and get another. The descent into the White River Valley branch just west of Kent was about the same.

tor had already entered the agricultural scene at White River. That factor was the cultivation of hops, a cash crop that would in the coming decade transform the valley's economy.

Historians disagree on who first introduced hops into King County in the late 1870s. One source claims that Richard Jeffs and James Crow first brought the roots in 1878 from the farm of the eminent Ezra Meeker of Puyallup, the neighboring river valley in Pierce County. Another earlier source states that Patrick Hayes first planted nine acres of hops on his farm in 1875, and that the following year C. M. Van Doren put in 20 acres. The *Daily Pacific Tribune* of Seattle noted on December 20, 1877, that grower Van Doren had devised a way to package and market small

With the resumption of settlement along White River in the 1860s came many citizen petitions to the King County Commissioners for road construction in the valley. A number of these roads had to be privately built, their maintenance later turned over to the county. Coal-mining activity in the nearby Renton and Newcastle area led to the construction of an important valley arterial from the bridge over Black River south through the Renton and Talbot mines to Langston's ferry. A plat for this road, commonly known as the County Road, was filed in August 1879, although it may have been laid out earlier. If conditions were good, valley farmers could take this wagon road as far downriver as Uncle Joe Foster's place at Black River Junction. From

Cable ferries, like this one in the Snoqualmie River area, were used to cross the White River in the 1870s. Big enough to hold a team and wagon plus passengers, the ferries were maneuvered from bank to bank by means of pulleys, cables, and manpower. Courtesy, Seattle Post-Intelligencer Collection, Museum of History and Industry

there a narrow-gauge railroad built for the coal industry in 1876 carried passengers all the way into Seattle.

Where east-west roads connected farms across the marshy valley floor, settlers resorted to corduroy or puncheon construction techniques. Slabs of cedar were laid across long poles, the spaces oftentimes filled in with dirt. Puncheon roads were infamous for their treachery, literal booby traps for horse's hoof and wagon wheel alike. But without such construction, valley roads were mired knee-deep in mud the better part of the year. In summer, this soft alluvial dirt turned to fine dust that enveloped and choked the hardy traveler.

Until 1883, there were no bridges across the White River. Overland sojourners had to ford the stream or make use of a canoe left at the bank by a property owner for just that purpose. By the 1870s, well-established ferry boat crossings helped tie together the growing network of valley roads. Powered by the river current, and maneuvered by pulley and cable, these ferries were simple wooden wagon scows large enough to transport a team and wagon. Several ferry crossings operated within the present-day city limits of Kent, and they are commemorated today by special markers placed along the riverbank by community organizations during the Bicentennial.

Mud, dust, and marshland, the inconvenience of crossings, and the treachery of puncheon roads made overland travel a poor second to water transport. White River itself was the valley's chief highway. As it had for centuries of aboriginal occupation, the river carried more than 90 percent of all traffic into and out of the valley. Pioneer fields and farmhouses were oriented toward its banks. People and farm animals, produce and "store-bought" goods, and news and mail floated up and down this pastoral corridor of commerce.

The earliest movement of people and goods along the water was by canoe. Indians performed this service for a nominal fee, or settlers themselves undertook the trip to market on Elliott Bay. Here they marketed farm products in exchange for a return haul of tools, clothing, or foodstuffs. When a cargo was particularly bulky, two canoes were lashed together by a platform on poles to form a rude barge.

Scow transport was introduced on the river by the early 1860s. Flat-bottom rafts much like the ferries in design, scows were poled or sailed from makeshift landings to trading points around Elliott Bay. Some were operated by farmers themselves, such as Patrick Hayes, Thomas Alvord, and Levi Smith. Thomas Alvord in particular seems to have built up a substantial if not entirely profitable scow trade almost immediately, putting up a sturdy landing and warehouse on his riverbank shortly after his arrival in 1859.

stern-first, all the way to Seattle. Rudders were of little use, so to keep the boat centered in the channel going downstream, each vessel dragged heavy chains off the bow. Seasons of low water were a special challenge, and many a steamer was beached in the mud, or stranded at low tide on the tideflats at Elliott Bay.

Like a train whistle across the plains, a steamboat signal up the winding White River Valley was an exciting, romantic sound. To isolated farm families it announced the arrival of civilization, a chance for social interaction and an exchange of goods. Schedules were rather flexible, dependent largely upon the need of any farmer along the river's shore. The steamers did not require a formal dock as such—in most instances, they could bump up against a soft bank and take on cargo across a plank. One such landing existed at David Neely's place where, his granddaughter reported in later years, the grandchildren gauged their visits to coincide with the scheduled arrival of the steamers.

Larger, more permanent landings where cargo from outlying farms might be stored for shipment were at Van Doren's, Langston's, and Alvord's landings. Langston's dock handled the shipment of tons of bales of hops from Ezra Meeker's local hop fields. At Alvord's, 150 tons of produce from his ranch and others upriver were loaded upon steamers each year. Except in times of exceedingly high water, Alvord's landing was the upriver terminus of the White River trade.

As prosperity in the valley blossomed with

Most scows operated perhaps once a month, and their arrivals in Seattle loaded down with White River produce were duly noted in the Seattle press. Colorful and functional, the *Minne Ha Ha,* the *Decatur,* and the *Black Diamond* lasted but a short while.

By 1870, river scows gave way to steamboats. As settlement along the valley floor increased, so too did the volume of river traffic. More than 15 steam-powered vessels operated over the course of the White River in a 17-year period. At the peak of this picturesque era, five or six sternwheelers regularly plied the stream, serving settlers from Alvord's ranch to the lower reaches of the Duwamish.

With its narrow, crooked channel and shallow, snag-choked bed, the White River inspired a special boat design. Flat-bottomed, narrow-hulled paddle-wheelers, some 100 feet from stem to stern, nosed their way along brushy banks the 20 or 30 miles upstream, only to back downstream

the hops boom in the late 1870s, White River folks enjoyed taking the steamers into Seattle for social outings, and Seattleites climbed aboard for light-hearted excursions up the peaceful, green valley. Some of the steamers were gaily painted and were leased upon occasion to private parties for special events and parties.

Though there were earlier steam-powered vessels on the river, the steamboat *Comet* was the first specifically adapted to the difficult channel. The *Comet*'s master, Captain Simon P. Randolph, pioneered the river trade by dragging the channel for snags in 1870, a work continued by later pilots.

Captain James J. Crow began his maritime career on the *Comet,* but by about 1882, profits from his hop ranch enabled him to purchase the *Lily,* the second of two vessels by that name. He piloted the *Lily* until the railroad became fully operational in 1887, outmoding river commerce for all time. Did Captain James Jeremiah Crow perceive the passing of an age when he ran the *Lily* aground at Alvord's landing and left her to rot? It was indeed the end of an era, the last phase of genuine pioneer transportation in the valley.

The linear settlement pattern of the White River country made frequent and casual social interaction among the neighboring farms a challenge. Though river travel was an efficient means of transportation, valley settlers of the 1860s and 1870s had difficulty congregating regularly for religious, educational, and social purposes. Nevertheless, a number of modern-day institutions in Kent trace their beginnings back to those pioneer decades when traveling to church or school could be an hours-long affair.

The first worship service conducted in the valley was a Methodist service hosted by Thomas Alvord, according to his logbook, in March 1861—the Reverend D.A. Spaulding preached a sermon. In the fall of that year, Julia Alvord's own brother, the Reverend R.C. Smith, delivered a second sermon at David A. Neely's home. For some time after that, alternate monthly services were held at the two homes. The Methodists soon

began using a log schoolhouse on the old Brannan homestead. In the summer, camp meetings were held from this location on the riverbank, and people from Seattle were encouraged to take free passage on a riverboat to come and participate. When the old school building was destroyed by fire, the Methodists began holding services in the vicinity of the White River post office. Here they constructed a building, perhaps one of the two churches listed at Maddocksville in *Choir's Directory* of 1878.

The White River Presbyterian Church was the first established in the Presbytery of Puget Sound. It was organized in July 1867, when the Reverend G.W. Sloan and a gathering of valley neighbors met together in another log schoolhouse at Langston's landing. The congregation was scattered, so services were sometimes held at the Willis School farther downriver, and sometimes at the Methodists' facility. It is said that Dr. Ballard, a charter member of the Presbyterian church, would drive a wagon and team over seven miles of rough roads to attend services at the Willis School.

Settlers of the Catholic faith organized even earlier when, in November 1864, Father Vary of Steilacoom came to minister to Irish families in the O'Brien area. Mass was held in private homes, among them that of pioneer farmer Patrick Hayes, until St. Bernard's Church was constructed in 1876 at O'Brien.

The White River Baptist Church was formed with 12 members in September 1874. The congregation was energetic, and under the leadership of the Reverend R. Weston they raised funds to erect a church building, quite probably at Maddocksville. It was dedicated in 1876.

Formal education began in the valley by 1869, when White River settlers organized as School District No. 3. Classes were first conducted in a log building on the river near John Langston's store. Miss Vina Gifford was the first teacher, and she counted among her 13 charges children from the Alvord, Graham, Crow, Willis, Blair, and Watson families.

Eventually Captain J.J. Crow donated an acre of his farm to the district and a brand-new schoolhouse was erected. Until 1881, valley children attended classes for only three summer months out of the year. Difficult transportation over mud-mired roads or on the swollen river, along with families' needs for seasonal help on the farm, made summer school the only practical schedule in those earliest days.

One of the first social-action organizations in the valley was a harbinger of progressive times to come. On January 17, 1874, *The Washington Stan-*

RIGHT: Adorned with flowers, the pupils of the Willis School near O'Brien stood solemnly for their portrait in 1902. The two-story wooden school accommodated students of all ages in the area north of Kent. Courtesy, White River Valley Historical Museum

BELOW: While a few larger schools were being built, numerous small, one-room schoolhouses, such as the Warnock School south of Kent, were still in use in the early 1900s. Students were assigned a rigorous schedule of classwork including math, reading, U.S. history, geography, language, and literature. The results of not studying were clearly evident. Courtesy, White River Valley Historical Museum

dard of Olympia announced that "Two granges of the Patrons of Husbandry have been organized in King County." Only one year after the formation of the national movement in Ohio, White River Grange #9 was founded by 23 farmers of the central valley. Dedicated to protecting the rights of agriculturalists, White River Grange #9 included among its charter members the pioneer names of Maddocks, Thomas, Lawton, Neely, McClellan, Benson, Langston, Nelson, Washburn, and others.

As the 1880s approached, the White River Valley brought to a close a colorful period of transition from wilderness to modern times. The days of potatoes to Seattle were over, and the stage had been set for monumental leaps forward in agriculture, transportation, and community identity. For some, the valley of opportunity had just begun to unfold.

The advent of the railroad marked the demise of the river sternwheelers, but inspired and encouraged growth along the railroad right-of-way in Kent. The railroad was faster and could carry more goods and people while connecting the White River Valley with neighboring cities and states. Engine Number 292, depicted here in 1908, served the White River Valley on the Northern Pacific Line. Courtesy, White River Valley Historical Museum

Forging a Community

The final decades of the nineteenth century took the fortunes of valley settlers on a roller coaster ride. The "hops craze" brought home the first fruits of real prosperity in the heady 1880s, and the coming of the railroad inspired a healthy optimism. The boom reached its peak in 1889 and 1890. All of Washington Territory celebrated the winning of statehood, and in the White River Valley, the town of Kent incorporated.

Within a few short years, fortunes plummeted as hops infestation, farm foreclosures, and business failures struck a heavy blow. Yet recovery was swift and sure, and by the turn of the century, the people of Kent once again found economic opportunity all around them.

No force shaped the landscape of the valley more completely in those decades than the advent of the railroad. With its construction, the age-old pattern of settlement along the meandering course of White River changed. Villages now sprang up in a linear pattern at strategic shipment points along the rail line. The village of Kent acquired its identity on the map and grew up on either flank of the railroad's right-of-way. But reliable commercial and passenger service through the valley did not come easily. Before the dust had settled, Kent-area farmers and businessmen displayed their mettle in a showdown with the Northern Pacific Railroad itself.

In 1881, the charismatic capitalist Henry Villard acquired control of the Northern Pacific, and arrived in Seattle with words of encouragement and intriguing promises. Among them was the notion of providing Seattle with a link to the main line by connecting an existing system in the Puyallup Valley with the Columbia and Puget Sound line between Seattle and Renton. The new track would run straight up the fertile White River Valley from Stuck Junction to Black River Junction. In exchange for this golden carrot, Villard extracted a pledge from Seattle's business community for free right-of-way along Seattle's waterfront. In the spring of 1883, the Northern Pacific awarded a contract for construction of the valley's new standard-gauge railroad to a Meyer Noonan Company. The contractor proceeded to assemble camps of Chinese laborers from Black River to Stuck Junction. Trusty steamboats hauled heavy rails and ties up and down the river. Thomas Alvord's logbooks reveal that he conducted a busy river trade that season supplying pork, rice, fish, and potatoes to the camps. He also leased horses and wagons to the contractors for the transport of surveyors, supervisors, laborers, and camps. Pioneer John Langston cleared eight miles of timbered right-of-way along the valley floor for the railroad that same spring.

Rail service commenced in the summer of 1883, but much to everyone's dismay, it was abruptly discontinued after just one month. Henry Villard fell from power in 1884, and after that, because no one seemed to know who owned the White River Valley branch line, it became known as the "Orphan Railroad." Frustration mounted as the months dragged on and the Northern Pacific gave no indication of any intention to activate the line.

That the prize so recently won should be taken away angered farmers and businessmen alike. In the summer of 1885, a public-spirited Kent man, nicknamed "Fog Horn Green" for his deep, booming voice, organized a mass meeting in Kent to discuss a means of reopening the Orphan Railroad. Seattle's leading citizens and elected officials, agents of the Northern Pacific, and valley farmers were all in attendance. A spokesman for the railroad explained to the assembled group that it was simply not profitable to operate a feeder line from nowhere to nowhere. Then Green called upon Judge Cornelius H. Hanford to speak. In later years, Hanford restated his impelling speech in these words:

Railroads are for public use. A railroad franchise imposes a duty to serve the public. This is a tangent; it takes a slice out of meadows, orchards and gardens; where houses and barns were obstructions they were removed to make way for a railroad. If you farmers did not consent to have your improved land cut into ribbons, the law of eminent domain gave consent, that means that public necessity is paramount to individual rights. After a railroad has been built it is a public highway, the public is entitled to use it; the same reason that justifies condemnation of land for public use likewise sanctions condemnation of an existing railroad that is not serving the public. If whoever has proprietary rights in this road cannot, or will not, operate it, you farmers can acquire possession of it rightfully and put it to work . . . I have here the figures showing that when it was operated for only one month its earnings in cash amounted to 50 per cent more than the expenses incurred for operation.

The sentiment of the assembly clearly supported this proposal. Suddenly, a telegram from New York arrived via a Northern Pacific attorney on horseback: the Orphan Railroad would be reactivated. Service to Seattle was restored by 1886, and the line was operated thereafter as the Puget Sound Shoreline Railroad.

In the heart of Kent between Gowe and Meeker streets, just east of the railroad tracks, a sturdy, two-story, framed depot with a pitched roof was erected, approximately where the Burlington Northern Station now stands. Pioneer Robert Ramsay contributed $250 for its construction. The depot became the center of the community, its visual focal point, and its symbolic link to markets on the Sound.

The founding of the town of Kent reflects to some degree the stop-and-start character of the valley's Orphan Railroad. Sporadic plattings and name changes through the 1880s soon led to stability and incorporation in 1890. Visualizing the development potential of land adjoining the newly completed rail line, the shrewd Seattle investor Henry Yesler first platted the "Town of Yesler" in March 1884, on land he acquired from Lewis

The Washington Central Improvement Company, a Kent real estate development firm, included two distinguished founding fathers of Kent. Seated, left to right, are A.T. Van de Vanter, first mayor; C.E. Guiberson, town councilman; and W.E. Harn; standing behind are W.B. Griffith and E.L. Whittmore. Courtesy, White River Valley Historical Museum

McMillan in payment of a debt. The Yesler plat was mostly wooded, but it encompassed much of what was to become downtown Kent, extending from Gowe Street to Willis, and from First Avenue west to Fifth.

East of Yesler's property was the 100-acre spread of James Henry Titus, a White River Valley farmer and blacksmith since 1872. The railroad right-of-way ran across Titus' farm, and around the time of its construction he began selling off lots adjacent to it for modest business development. A store, saloon, post office, and hotel were in place by the close of 1884.

Was there concern on the part of local residents that the outside investor Yesler's name might stick? Perhaps so, for the hotel, the post office, and the first Odd Fellows lodge in town all assumed

ABOVE: *The men of the Kent Fire Department were unable to save Fred's Place, a First Avenue saloon, as it burned to the ground around 1900. Wearing rain slickers and southwestern hats, and working with shovels and a hand-pulled hose cart, the volunteers had a nearly impossible task when dry wooden structures were engulfed in flames. Courtesy, White River Valley Historical Museum*

LEFT: *Standing on the corner of Second and Gowe streets, the bell tower of City Hall was a distinctive land-mark for Kent residents in 1918. The two-story wooden structure housed the fire department on the first floor and the town council on the second floor. Courtesy, White River Valley Historical Museum*

the name "Titusville." Titusville was not listed in any directories of the 1880s, but the name persisted in popular terminology for most of the decade, and is recalled in newspaper and journal articles of the period. The post office name was changed in 1887. "Titusville House" and "Titusville Hotel" are last listed in the directories of 1888 and 1889, respectively.

FACING PAGE: Martin Nelson, his family, and livestock all posed for this photo taken during the hop boom era of the 1880s. The hop kiln, or drier, is on the right, and a direct ramp to the storage shed is on the left. The Nelson farm was located near O'Brien. Courtesy, White River Valley Historical Museum

BELOW: During the hop boom, Native Americans from the surrounding countryside would travel to the hop fields. Families would set up camp and pick hops throughout the harvest season. A hop picker could make up to $3 a day, depending on the laborer's expertise. Courtesy, Special Collections Division, University of Washington Libraries

The railroad is believed to have been the first to make use of the name "Kent." Some say the eminent Ezra Meeker of the neighboring Puyallup Valley first suggested the name, envisioning a hops culture in the White River Valley that would rival the county of Kent in England. Others claim the name originated with a railroad employee who first dispatched boxcars from Stuck Junction for White River hops.

Whatever its origin, by the year 1888 the name Kent appears to have been embraced by its citizenry. In July 1888, John Alexander and Ida Guiberson filed the first plat of the town of "Kent." This plat, which extended three blocks south of Willis Street and three blocks east of the railroad's right-of-way, was not destined to become the center of

town. "Kent" is listed for the first time as a distinct community in R.L. Polk's *Puget Sound Directory* of 1888. The description it provides paints a revealing picture of the flourishing settlement on the eve of its incorporation:

KENT. A village on the Puget Sound Shore R.R. . . . settled in 1883. Lumber, hops, and farm produce are shipped. The Kent Milling Company have a sawmill with a capacity of 20,000 feet in 10 hours, and are building another . . . There are two general stores, a drug store and a Methodist Church . . . Charles E. Guiberson, postmaster.

An expanding economy and unprecedented growth in population spurred additional townsite development in 1889. The Washington Central Improvement Company, George M. Van Doren, president, platted the remainder of the Titus farm, extending buildable lots east from the railroad to Kennebeck Avenue, and south from James Street to Willis Street. In 1890 the Kent Land Company, comprised of Captain J.J. Crow,

J.C. Merrifield, M.M. Morrill, and W.J. Shinn, bought up the wooded Yesler addition and cleared and platted it, rounding out the core of the town west of the railroad tracks. A flurry of further additions in 1889-1890 essentially completed the boundaries of the early townsite.

In May 1890, citizens of the thriving community of Kent presented a petition to the Commissioners of King County, requesting authority to hold an election to incorporate and elect officers. The population of the town proper was 763. An election was duly held on May 22 at the offices of Crow and Shinn, with J.H. Titus serving as inspector. According to the official canvas there were 107 votes in favor of incorporation and 22 votes opposed. Kent can thus claim distinction as the first municipality in King County outside the City of Seattle to incorporate.

Aaron T. Van de Vanter, elected as Kent's first mayor, enjoyed a long and distinguished career in public service. A hop farmer, real estate developer, and civic activist, Van de Vanter soon went on to serve as a senator in the Washington

State Legislature. When his term expired, he ran successfully for sheriff of King County and was known for his effective capture of 23 escaped prisoners, the largest jail break in county history. A devoted agriculturist and horse breeder, Van de Vanter was one of the organizers and early managers of the King County Fair Association, as well as the largest grower and shipper of asparagus on Puget Sound.

Mayor Van de Vanter called the first regular meeting of Kent's newly elected town council on May 28, 1890. Councilmen William C. Faulkner, Charles E. Guiberson, James C. Merrifield, Robert Ramsay, and Dr. Julien Soule were present.

Council meetings were held at William Shinn's office until late 1891, when a handsome new town hall and fire station on Gowe Street near Second opened its doors.

There was much work to be accomplished by the fledgling town government. Council minutes and ordinances from the first decade, still preserved at Kent City Hall, provide a colorful summary of small-town living. Mayor Van de Vanter started matters off on the right foot by submitting Ordinance #1, establishing a fine of five dollars for each council member who failed to attend a regular council meeting. Ordinance #8 set a high

In 1887, after pedaling 16 miles from Seattle to Kent, the men of the Queen City Bicycle Club posed for this photo on the house of Aaron Van de Vanter. Van de Vanter, a farmer and dairyman, was elected Kent's first mayor in 1890. Courtesy, White River Valley Historical Museum

moral standard for the community by prohibiting lewd dress, saloons on Sunday, houses of ill fame, driving a horse or mule more than eight miles per hour, and failure to assist an officer of the law when requested. Ordinance #33 protected the town's landscaping by outlawing the hitching of horses to ornamental shade trees on streets or public squares. The streets of Kent were kept safe for the citizenry by Ordinance #73, which prevented horses, mules, geldings, mares, jacks, sheep, hogs, shoats, and pigs from running at large.

Police protection was evidently not a pressing need in those times. Although a town marshal was hired in 1890 for 75 dollars per month, his salary was reduced the following year, and eliminated altogether in 1898. Not surprisingly, the marshal resigned that year. Nonetheless, plenty of ordinances were passed in the name of public safety, establishing speed limits for horse-drawn wagons and bicycles, prohibiting Chinese bombs or firecrackers in the center of town, and outlawing the hopping of railroad cars in motion.

By 1892, Kent's city directory boasted of the town's "efficient and well-organized fire department." High above city hall, a shingled fire tower with an alarm bell overlooked the town. Town council minutes of 1893 indicate a recurring concern over the condition of the fire equipment, which at first consisted of nothing but a chemical cart. By 1896, however, the local newspaper reported that Kent had developed a separate water supply system with 80 pounds pressure in the mains for fire fighting, and "a good volunteer fire company, well drilled and equipped with buckets, ladders, hose and carts."

The civic progress and economic vitality of early-day Kent was made possible by "the Golden Age of Hops." The White River Valley was not alone in experiencing this phenomenon—intensive cultivation of hops extended far into Oregon and northern California. The crop grew prolifically in the rich soil and mild climate of western Washington Territory. Inexpensive to establish and high in average yield per acre, hops were considered a sure road to financial independence. Although annual prices were determined by the eastern and European market, White River farmers might expect in a good year to earn $400 per acre or more. For a period of 12 years, as agricultural land values soared, growers around Kent cleared acreage as fast as they were able, putting in hops and reaping the seemingly limitless profits.

Native Americans did the bulk of the picking at harvest time. In the late summer, thousands of

Indians young and old began their journey to the hop fields. From all around Puget Sound, from British Columbia and east of the Cascades, they made their colorful way by canoe and horseback. A prominent grower of the period wrote:

When fairly settled down to it, they are inveterate and reliable workers, going to the hop field as soon as they can see to work, carrying their dinners with them, and remaining until pitch dark. Experts among them make as high as $3 a day in some cases, but, taking the average, only about $1.25 a day. The question of questions with the hop growers is, Will enough come? If so, will they arrive in time? From a supposed short supply of help timid growers become scared and begin to bid up and run after fresh arrivals. The Indians are quick to perceive the situation, and ready to profit by the anxiety of growers and drive the best bargain possible.

Hops transformed the countryside surrounding Kent with the distinctive architecture of the hopyard. Wooden hop kilns or driers, on the average 20 feet square, silhouetted the skyline with their steeply pitched, hipped roofs, crowned by cupolas for the release of steam and fumes from the drying hops. Exterior ramps provided access to the

high, latticed drying floors. Two-story storerooms or warehouses, sometimes flanked by kilns, and press rooms for the baling completed the assemblage.

Substantial income and good credit enabled White River hop farmers to construct fine new residences in the 1880s. Two- and three-story framed dwellings with Italianate bracketed cornices and Queen Anne-styled bay windows went up on the farm and in town. Many a family ordered new furnishings, china, and linens from stores in Seattle. Investment in real estate and businesses in Kent

ABOVE: Frances DeSmet and Mr. Carlson are depicted here at the corner of Meeker and Central streets on their way to the Carnation Milk Condensary around 1905. Pulling a full load of milk cans, the horses are covered with netting to protect them from persistent flies. Courtesy, White River Valley Historical Museum

BELOW: E.A. Stuart founded the Pacific Coast Condensed Milk Company in Kent in 1899. Located on First and Meeker streets, the condensary turned out 3,000 cans of milk daily, and became a worldwide distributor of Carnation Condensed Milk. Courtesy, White River Valley Historical Museum

accelerated during this decade of prosperity. The population of carpenters, laborers, and shopkeepers in Kent increased dramatically.

In the early 1890s the unthinkable occurred. A plague of hops lice infested the fields of western Washington. Within a few short years the industry was ruined. The rapid decline is reflected in "Hops News and Notes" in the local newspaper, the *White River Journal.* Even as the column diminished in size, the newspaper carried advertisements for spray pumps and insecticides, including whale oil soap and quassia chips. Against the hops louse and a simultaneous price depression, hop growers fought a losing battle. Among those who faced financial ruin was Ezra Meeker, the largest hop dealer in Washington Territory whose acreage on the outskirts of Kent was widely known. Meeker spoke for many valley farmers when he remarked, "I went to bed wealthy and I got up next morning a pauper."

Economic catastrophe reached even greater proportions when ripple effects of the Panic of 1893 struck the valley. Throughout the mid-1890s, the Kent town council enacted belt-tightening measures designed to keep the community's head above water. Many valley farms were foreclosed in payment of debt. In April 1896, pioneer Thomas Alvord was declared insolvent and his ranch and stock were sold at public auction. In October of the same year, a small note in the *White River Journal* announced "the unfortunate failure of the bank at this place." Kent's population fell from a peak of 1,000 to little over 600, and property values plummeted 40 to 80 percent.

In the desperate period of readjustment which followed the hops failure, a new form of agriculture rose to the fore. As hop fields reverted to pas-

Huge logs were pulled by horses over a skid road to the mill pond of the Kent Lumber Company, located at the base of East Hill. The lumbermen would handle the heavy logs with fork-like peaveys and long, pointed pikes. These loggers are depicted in 1903. Courtesy, White River Valley Historical Museum

tures, dairy farming quickly gained ascendance. Profitable dairying had long taken place in the valley—farmers like Thomas Alvord had maintained large herds—but its influence had waned in the 1880s while hops was "king" and acreage was at a premium. By the 1890s, the burgeoning population of Seattle and Tacoma created a soaring demand for fresh milk and dairy products. Most significantly, the railroad now allowed quick shipment to market, reducing the risk of loss by spoilage. Fresh milk commanded high prices, and although a dairy farmer's initial investment was great, he could realize a substantial profit. In 1898, the Kent town council granted a franchise and special water privileges to the Washington Condensed Milk Company for a condensing plant in town. When the enterprise failed a year and a half later, a new company came forward "proposing to reopen the Condenser," and requesting similar concessions on light and water rates. This new outfit was Elbridge A. Stuart's Pacific Coast Condensed Milk Company, soon to become the Carnation Milk Company, a world-class industry.

Stuart would later write of his first operation at Kent:

We located a small plant at Kent, Washington which had been established for the processing of sweetened condensed milk. The company had failed and the machinery and equipment were bought at Sheriff's sale by the First National Bank of Helena, Montana. We purchased the equipment for the sum of $5000 and rented the realty. We had to reassemble the machinery and make certain additions so as to adapt it to the processing of evaporated milk. While we were preparing the plant for operation we employed a high class Swiss dairyman, nicknamed "Cheese John," who worked with the local dairymen educating them as to the method of producing a high quality fresh milk so that we could produce a high quality evaporated milk. On the 6th of September 1899, we received about 5800 pounds of fluid milk which we processed into 55 cases of evaporated milk.

The Pacific Coast Condensed Milk Company's establishment at Kent heralded the rise of the King County dairy industry, and signified a welcome upswing in the economy. With Kent at its center, the valley of opportunity entered the twentieth century riding high once again on a new wave of optimism.

to the Northern Pacific line. The mill was prosperous and widely advertised as the largest concern between Seattle and Tacoma, offering for sale "rustic, flooring, pickets, telegraph and telephone poles, rough and dressed lumber, bridge timbers, and car materials."

Along First Avenue and Railroad Avenue, a commercial center of false-fronted frame buildings grew up. Mercantile, feed, and grocery stores, and blacksmith and specialty shops filled the storefronts, while professional offices and small manufactories occupied second-floor spaces. Among the latter were a cigar factory, a small brewery, and a furniture factory.

Although its economy was firmly rooted in agriculture, Kent was not without other forms of business and industry, many of which were able to weather the turbulent 1880s and 1890s. Logging, lumber milling, and shingle milling were major employers of Kent area workers from an early date. The pioneer lumber business was founded by Peter Saar in 1883, and was later operated by Albert E. and Lysander Smith as The Kent Mill Company, and still later, the Kent Lumber Company. This firm logged off much of East Hill and established several mills, one at O'Brien and at least two in Kent. Built in 1890, the plant at Mill Creek was soon connected by a spur down Smith Street

Kent's first bank opened in 1890, capitalized at $25,000. Thomas Devine served as its president, as well as president of the Kent Board of Trade, a fledgling chamber of commerce organized in 1891. When the bank failed in 1896, M.M. Morrill, former mercantile and meat market proprietor, organized the First National Bank of Kent, which opened its doors for business soon afterward.

Kent supported an astonishing array of commercial establishments during those prosperous years. Among them were a bakery, meat market, restaurant, saloon, several hotels, a grocery, and a general merchandise store; a florist, a jeweler's, a milliner's, and a pharmacy; a stationery/bookshop,

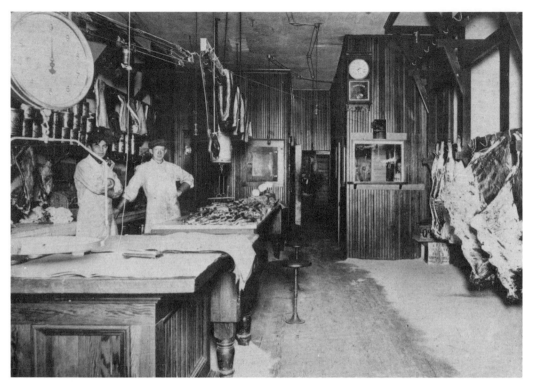

ABOVE: *In 1915 Dunn's Meat Market welcomed customers with fresh chops and sausage rolls. Beef and pork halves hung from hooks awaiting selection and fresh sawdust was piled on the floor for sanitation purposes. Behind the youthful butchers, shelves held buckets of lard for cooking. Courtesy, White River Valley Historical Museum*

FACING PAGE: *With newly paved streets and brick buildings, First Avenue was a main business block for Kent residents in 1910. The First National Bank of Kent, with its prominent arched windows, stood on the corner of First and Gowe streets. These same buildings are in use today. Courtesy, White River Valley Historical Museum*

1890. This in turn was succeeded by the *White River Journal,* "Published to Do Good and Make Money," W.W. Corbet, editor. The *Journal* would continue as the voice of Kent for many years to come.

Kent's utility systems rapidly took shape during this time period. The Kent Water and Light Company, consisting of Shinn, Crow, and Guiberson, first piped water into town from a spring above Crow's farm in 1888. Electric lights came to town in 1890, courtesy of J.T. Jones' generating plant. The town of Kent acquired both of those utilities in 1892. The generating plant proved difficult to operate in the depression years—even the wood supply was a continuing concern to the Kent town council. A complete shutdown was debated in 1893, but in the end the council settled for turning off the streetlights on moonlit nights. By 1896, Kent had telephone connections to Seattle, Tacoma, and Olympia.

a furniture store, a cigar shop, and a piano/organ dealership. Boots and shoes, saddlery and harnesses, agricultural implements, and hardware could all be purchased in the thriving business district.

An equally wide range of services could be had. In Kent, one could retain the services of an attorney, an assayer, a doctor, a photographer, a dentist, a tailor, or a barber. There were printing, laundry, dressmaking, and blacksmithing services for hire. Dealers in insurance, real estate, hops, and livestock did business in town, as did a contractor, a plasterer, a cabinet maker, and a carpenter.

Several newspapers were started up in those pivotal years. The *Kent Recorder,* Beriah Brown, editor, was forerunner of the *Advertiser* established in

Economic conditions had little impact upon the progress of Kent's cultural life in the last decades of the century. Education took a giant step forward when voters of the school district authorized a bond issue to fund construction of the Valley School in Kent in 1890. It was a handsome two-story structure with arched gate entries on either side, wide banks of transomed windows, and a seating capacity of 400 students. In the mid-1890s, the school hired as principal Charles F. Allan. Over an 11-year career, Allan worked to upgrade the school's curriculum, instituting night school courses for older students, extending the school year to a full nine months, establishing nine grade levels, and

ABOVE: The men of the International Order of Odd Fellows Band posed for this photo around 1915 before playing to a patriotic gathering at the city bandstand. Located near the Northern Pacific tracks, with the two-story depot in the distance, the city park was the center of festivities for holiday activities. Courtesy, White River Valley Historical Museum

FACING PAGE: The bicycle craze of the 1890s afflicted the women as well as the men. These six young ladies from Kent were appropriately attired in casual dress and skimmer hats for a leisurely ride in the country. Courtesy, White River Valley Historical Museum

byterians both moved into Kent in 1889 and put up new buildings. In the following two years, a Protestant Episcopal Church and a Scandinavian Lutheran Church were organized. These five congregations formed the nucleus of the community's spiritual and social life throughout the hard times that followed.

Fraternal organizations and women's groups gained prominence in these formative decades as well. Titusville Lodge #34 of the International Order of Odd Fellows was founded in 1886, and Adina Rebekah Lodge #27 in 1890. The Odd Fellows made a lasting contribution to Kent when they established the first cemetery in town. Hillcrest Burial Park, still in operation today, was developed on four acres of land at the crest of East Hill, purchased from the Washington Central Improvement Company. Other organizations working toward community betterment in the 1890s were the Masons, the Woodmen of the World, the Order of Princes, and the Women's Christian Temperance Union.

Throughout this period, the pages of the local *White River Journal* reflected the social life of the era when church, school, and club activities filled most families' leisure moments. During 1893, the Kent Chautauqua Circle met weekly for cultural stimulation. Young people of the Episcopal Guild and St. James Club held a "club and saucer social" with dinner and dancing at the Brick Hotel. At the Willis School on Friday nights, stereopticon views were shown. The Kent W.C.T.U. hosted the annual King County convention at the Presbyterian Church. In January

vastly increasing the average daily attendance.

Kent's churches made great strides in the 1880s and 1890s, when a number of the pioneer congregations moved into town from old locations along White River. The Methodist Episcopal Church was erected on First Avenue in 1883 with monies raised in a fund drive begun by Thomas Alvord. For its construction the steamboat *Lily* hauled lime, paint, and nails upriver from Schwabacher's hardware store in Seattle. When the railroad line became fully operational, the noise of the passing trains shook the church and drowned out the sermon so completely that the location had eventually to be moved. The Baptists and Pres-

1894, the Odd Fellows hosted a Grand Ball at their meeting hall with dinner and dancing until 3 a.m. In honor of the occasion, the Auburn Cornet Band arrived by train and marched in the streets. All manner of Christmas parties, concerts, and recitations were held at the churches around town; the trimming of the town's official Christmas tree was sponsored annually by the Methodist Episcopals. In the summer of 1895, the Ladies Aid Society of the Kent Baptist Church held a "bouquet social" on the church lawn, and the W.C.T.U. sponsored an ice cream social.

Private homes, too, were the scene of parties and balls on a scale not often repeated in more modern times. Thirty young people danced the night away in the third-story ballroom of Captain J.J. Crow in December 1894. The following winter, dozens of guests from Auburn to Seattle gathered at the home of Moses Maddocks on White River. There they enjoyed a lavish midnight supper and dancing resumed until 4 a.m.

The performing arts were valued in Kent from an early date. Odd Fellows Hall served as

the town "opera house," seating 500 people. By 1896, Kent had organized its own Cornet Band to perform at community events.

Sports were equally as important. In the spring of 1895, the Kent town baseball team played the Muckleshoot team. Horse racing was taken seriously and for a time in the 1880s and early 1890s, when Kent hosted the annual county fair, its racetrack and fairgrounds were popular attractions. Kent was headquarters of the State Gun Club, and home of the "Betsey Rod and Gun Club."

No pastime seems to have been as wholeheartedly embraced in Kent in the 1890s as bicycling. The pages of the *White River Journal* were filled increasingly with ads for the marvelous new machines, some brands marketed in town: Ben-Hur, White, Monarch, Sterling, and Back-from-the-Hunt. The Kent Bicycle Club gained repeated attention by the town council, and in 1896 opened a new quarter-mile racetrack. On October 10 of that year a Grand Cycle Meet was held at the new track, widely advertised and open to cyclists from Kent, Auburn, Black Dia-

mond, and the entire valley. Eleven races for all age groups and skill levels were announced and a long list of prizes such as a cyclometer, a volume of Byron's poems, and an elegant pocket knife were donated. Every prominent citizen and businessman turned out to serve as starter, timer, or judge. Music was provided by the Kent Cornet Band, and the event was climaxed with a big dance in the evening. The Grand Cycle Meet brought Kent together in the spirit of better days to come.

The Pacific Highway, completed in 1915, ran the length of King County. This portion of the highway, constructed of wooden planks on a graded dirt and gravel bed, was tried out by members of the Seattle and Tacoma auto clubs. Courtesy, Museum of History and Industry, Seattle, Washington

Progressive Times

All around Kent and throughout the Puget Sound region, the first decades of the twentieth century brought accelerated environmental and social change. In the White River Valley, farmers and engineers joined forces in a continuing effort to tame the land. By 1920, the people of Kent enjoyed the most modern of transportation systems. Even as dairy farming stabilized the valley's economy, its social structure expanded and evolved with the influx of new ethnic groups. In the spirit of the age, farmers strengthened their political and economic clout in a resurgence of the grange movement, and townsfolk rallied together to make Kent a "progressive" little city.

One of the earliest manipulations of the landscape was designed to provide flood relief in the northern valley. The farmers of Kent, O'Brien, and Orillia banded together in 1906 to form King County Drainage District No. One. An 11-mile canal, 28 feet by 14 feet, was dug from Kent to Renton Junction with an east-west ditch at Orillia and laterals at Kent. The drainage system worked, albeit imperfectly, to ease the annual destructive overflow of the Black and Duwamish rivers, whose waters might cause back-up as far south as Kent.

Drainage canals proved grossly inadequate in 1906, the year of the Great Flood. The magnitude of that natural disaster would soon result in the permanent redesign of the valley's river system. The fall rains had been particularly heavy that season. By mid-November, stream beds and river channels, blocked with debris, overflowed their banks. From Meadows Race Track on the middle Duwamish all the way to Auburn, the valley became a veritable lake traversable only by rowboat. Train tracks and roadbeds were inundated and bridges washed away. At Kent, the waters rose to two feet in houses on the west side of town, and reached as far east as Third Avenue. The city water system and the milk condenser's sewer were knocked out of service.

Most significantly, the raging White River tore away a narrow neck of land that separated it from the Stuck River near Auburn. As it had in distant centuries past, the White shifted the whole of its flow south into the channel of the Puyallup River. Farms in the vicinity of Kent and Auburn experienced almost immediate relief, while the Puyallup Valley filled with water from bluff to bluff.

Over the Christmas holidays of 1906, valley landowners, county officials, and railroad men met in Auburn to discuss a course of action. Out of that meeting came a board of inquiry, chaired by Aaron T. Van de Vanter, former first mayor of Kent. Major Hiram Chittenden of the U.S. Army Corps of Engineers prepared a report on behalf of the board, in which he recommended that the White River be permanently channeled south to the Puyallup.

Various reports and studies followed over a seven-year period until 1913, when King and Pierce county commissioners entered into a joint agreement for river improvement. Work began in January 1914. A reinforced concrete dam at Auburn diverted the waters of the White River south, and a massive drift barrier of concrete and steel helped to control the problem of log jams. Eventually, the channels of the Stuck and Puyallup rivers were deepened, widened, and straightened.

This landmark engineering project had particular import to the people of Kent. To begin with, the historic White River Valley was technically no longer the White. Instead, the waters of Green River, a former tributary, occupied the old meandering channel to Elliott Bay. Although Major Chittenden recommended extension of the term "Duwamish" up the length of the stream, it was the Green River which ever so gradually lent its name by popular usage to the valley. With its flow now cut in half, the new stream was slower, tamer, and less prone to regular destructive flooding.

The new century ushered in a long-awaited

ABOVE: Steam tractors and rollers, along with a grader, were some of the construction vehicles used in paving part of the West Valley Highway around 1912. Asphalt-type surfaces were put down as an experiment to evaluate how well they would wear in traffic and in various weather conditions. Courtesy, White River Valley Historical Museum

FACING PAGE, TOP: The Kent Interurban depot was located at Meeker Street and Sixth Avenue. The building featured a waiting area, offices, and a living area for train crews. The car barn and repair shops nearby were part of the Kent headquarters for this unique mode of transportation. This image dates around 1920. Courtesy, White River Valley Historical Museum

FACING PAGE, BOTTOM: The Ed Oies family proudly displayed their new Model T Ford in 1914. Although the first automobile arrived in 1905, it was 1913 before a car dealership, the Kent Motor Car Company, opened its doors in Kent and gave valley residents a convenient opportunity to purchase a motorized vehicle. Courtesy, White River Valley Historical Museum

crews, trainmen, station crews, and dispatchers. When an Interurban pulled into Kent city limits from the north, the brakeman scurried to shift power from the exposed third rail to an overhead trolley line. The motorman brought the train to a stop, bells clanging, at the Kent depot on Meeker Street and Sixth. The station was a substantial two-story frame building with a covered porch on three sides. Inside, the depot housed the company superintendent's offices; a bunkroom for trainmen complete with lockers, pool table, and library; the dispatcher's office; and a waiting room and ticket office. A large express and baggage room featured a freight track that ran right into the center of the building between platforms.

As the train pulled out of the station, off to the left one could see the Interurban's principal car barn, a one-story wooden structure with storage space for 16 cars. All cars on the Seattle-Tacoma run originated and tied up here, except in the worst of weather. Near the car barn, the busy repair shops could service up to 12 cars at one time. The Kent yards were further equipped with a substation and passing track. Besides offering stable employment to a segment of Kent's population, the Interurban provided a first-class passenger and freight service that is enviable by today's standards. High-speed trains called at Kent with frequency—by 1906 there were 34 stops daily at the town depot. A "limited" could reach Seattle or Tacoma from Kent in less than 35 minutes. Commuters, schoolchildren, and tourists alike enjoyed the smooth and scenic ride. Although passenger service formed the backbone of the Interurban's business, it also commonly hauled freight. Carry-

advancement in public transportation—the electric railway. Many a Kent community meeting in the 1890s had talked up the desirability of such a system, but the dream did not become reality until September 1902, when the first shiny green Brill cars rolled down from Seattle to Tacoma and back again. To the delight of local businessmen, the Puget Sound Electric Railway established its sizeable operating headquarters at Kent. For over a quarter-century, the Interurban gave employment to dozens of Kent residents as maintenance

ing timber and coal, fresh milk and farm produce, the Puget Sound Electric Railroad gave the valley's conventional steam railroads (the Northern Pacific, and by 1910, the Chicago, Milwaukee and Puget Sound) a serious run for their money.

On the heels of the ultra-modern Interurban came the age of the automobile. The first car in Kent appeared about 1905 and is said to have been a one-cylinder "Brush," the proud possession of Jim Finley, Northern Pacific depot agent. Dr. Owen Taylor was one of the early owners as well. The rules of the road were still ill-defined, but the courteous motorist was expected to pull over and turn off his machine on narrow country roads so as not to spook an oncoming horse and wagon. Until the advent of service stations, drivers bought their gasoline at the local drugstore. In 1913, Robert Shinn opened the town's first automobile agency, the Kent Motor Car Company. Shinn offered the latest model Chalmers and Maxwells as well as old reliable Fords. The same year, the McGhee Auto Company on Meeker Avenue introduced the sporty Overland for $1,100, completely equipped.

With the advent of the automobile came trucks, buses, jitneys, or autostages, and all manner of motorized vehicles. County engineers began to search seriously for a method of hard-surfaced road construction. The West Valley Highway, constructed in 1911-1912, was an experiment in "Warrenite" asphalt construction from its origin near Meadows Race Track south into Kent. From Kent to Auburn, the county contracted for a hard brick "cobblestone" pavement. Portions of the old brick highway, too slippery to compete successfully with macadam or asphaltic surfaces, remained exposed into the 1950s.

The 1915 completion of the Pacific Highway through King County, of which the West Valley Road was a part, was a turning point in valley transportation, signaling the beginning of decline for rail travel. There was no looking back. Public attention turned to the need for good auto roadways. In the vanguard of the citizen movement at the local, state, and national level was Frank Terrace, well-known Orillia dairyman. Along with railroad man Sam Hill, Terrace founded the "King County Good Roads Association," and went on himself to become vice president of both the Pacific Highway Association and the Washington State Good Roads Association.

In the countryside of western Washington, dairy farming flourished in the first decades of the new century. Promotional literature of the period touted dairying as the predominant agricultural activity in King County, and so it was.

ABOVE: In the early 1900s the Standard Dairy was owned by Erick Sanders and L.A. Oien and encompassed 603 acres. Oien managed the dairy herd, which was housed in the largest barn in the valley. In the 1930s the farm was purchased and operated by the Smith Brothers Dairy. Courtesy, White River Valley Historical Museum

FACING PAGE: Farm wagons laden with milk cans lined up to unload their liquid cargo at the Carnation Condensary in 1900. This view of the condensary looks east along Meeker Street with East Hill in the background. Courtesy, White River Valley Historical Museum

. . . it is hard to conceive a section of the universe in which nature has more bountifully provided for the dairyman than in King County, Washington, where logged off lands are to be purchased at low cost, where the grass is green twelve months in the year, and where a great city consumes thousands of pounds of milk and butter daily, and great condensers prepare the product of the dairy for consumption in the lumber and mining camps of Washington, Alaska, and British Columbia . . . Dairying is one of the principal resources about which many of the leading towns of King County have been built. In the fertile White River Valley, Kent and Auburn are each the location of a large condenser, while O'Brien, Thomas, Christopher and Orillia, near-by places, are the scene of much trade in dairy products.

Around Kent, dairy farms dotted the valley floor and proliferated on the hilly plateau to the

Meeker and Smith streets. The complex included a lab, solder house, office, can plant, and warehouse.

Each day, Kent farmers strained fresh milk into large 10-gallon containers and set them out on roadside platforms for pickup by one of the many condenser route wagons. Back in town, the milk wagons lined up two deep at the condensery to unload. The farmers' cans were then washed and sterilized at no cost, and sent back on the return trip. Many Kent citizens remember milky wash water running through gutters along the streets of town.

Relations were not always smooth between the condensery and its suppliers. Dairymen occasionally discovered that their milk would fetch higher prices at Borden's condensery in Auburn or on the fresh milk market in Seattle via the Interurban line. In November 1906, officials of

east. Kent's great condensery, the Pacific Coast Condensed Milk Company, bought up most local milk for the production of "Carnation Cream." Its business expanded rapidly, and by 1910 the firm employed 250 people, and paid out an average of $1,000 per day in monthly checks to the farming community. In its heyday, the plant occupied two city blocks, bounded by First and Second, and

the condensery met with agitated farmers. Company president Elbridge Stuart himself explained the costs involved in production, and flatly refused to compete with Borden's. He concluded by reminding all those present that if he could not do business in Kent, he would move the condensery elsewhere. The local newspaper sided with management, pointing out:

The Condenser is the main support of this portion of the valley, since all attempts at gardening has met with failure on account of the inability to place it on the market at any profit. Until something that can handle the produce of this fertile region can be in operation, the Condenser is and will be the main source of revenue.

The Pacific Coast Condensed Milk Company had labor problems as well. A major strike in 1916 forced the closure of the milk processing operation at Kent, the same year the firm's name was changed to Carnation Milk Products. But the manufacture of tin cans for Carnation's expanding chain of northwest condenseries continued at Kent through the 1920s. At its peak, the plant turned out 50,000 tin cans a day.

By the close of World War I, dairying had become distinctly less profitable for valley farmers. Production had increased to meet demand, and when the war ended, prices fell drastically. Many Kent dairymen were forced to sell out at a loss.

Berry growing expanded concurrently with dairying in the period from 1900 to 1920. From Kent to Auburn, as far as the eye could see, lay field after field of loganberries, raspberries, blackberries, strawberries, currants, and boysenberries. Berrying offered a reliable cash return on smaller tracts too limited in acreage for dairy herds.

Dependent as it was upon seasonal labor, cool storage, and rapid shipment to market, berrying was a somewhat fragile enterprise. To handle distribution most efficiently, local farmers banded together to form the White River Berry Growers' Association, with offices in Auburn. As early as 1907, Kent attempted to attract a berry cannery of its own, but it was slow in coming. One hundred growers and businessmen met one evening early in May 1916 to discuss the possibility of erecting a cooling plant and berry shipping station at Kent. The following year, a small cannery operation started up. In the 1920s, when wormy infestations attacked the fields, berrying suffered a decline, and was soon replaced by the gradual rise of truck gardening.

Vegetables and fruits had always grown abundantly in the rich valley soil. But in the early 1900s, Kent area farmers faced increasing difficulty in marketing their fresh produce in Seattle, where wholesale dealers on Western Avenue defrauded the producer and kept consumer prices sky high. A Kent farmer reported:

I went to Seattle one day last summer and asked Western Avenue dealers what they would pay for a certain fine variety of cherries I saw on the sidewalk . . . They said they would give me fifteen cents a box. I went home, packed up better cherries than I saw for sale there and next day received five cents a box—

ABOVE: Kisa Okuna Iseri, second from the right, was photographed with her family in Japan in 1900. She later immigrated to Washington State, where, in 1907, she married Mat Iseri of the Thomas area south of Kent. The White River Valley area attracted many immigrant Japanese who took the opportunity to establish farms on leased land. Courtesy, Mae Iseri Yamada Collection

FACING PAGE: Both strawberries and cane berries thrived in the soil and climate of the White River Valley. These Japanese farm families posed in 1918 with raspberries freshly picked from the canes in the background. Berries were first sold as fresh produce and later processed into jellies, jams, and preserves at the Libby, McNeill and Libby factory. Courtesy, Mae Iseri Yamada Collection

not enough to pay for packing and shipping. When the cherries got there the commission men had me, and they knew it and put on the screws. The price of cherries hadn't gone down. It was just a case—a plain case—of stealing from the farmer.

In response to this situation, Seattle's Pike Place Market opened in 1907. Now valley growers could load up a wagon or truckload of fresh produce, travel to Seattle and sell directly to the consumer, and return that night with a pocketful of silver. Truck or garden produce, grown economically on small acreage, often by tenant or immigrant farmers, awaited a golden age still to come in the postwar decades of the 1920s and 1930s.

Kent area farmers participated in the regional rejuvenation of the grangers' movement in the early 1900s, as well as the formation of cooperative processing, distribution, and retail opera-

tions. Meridian Grange, White River Grange #238, Valley Central Grange, Thomas Grange, and East Hill Grange all came into being between 1908 and 1921. Dissatisfied with their treatment at the hands of Kent merchants, valley grange members joined forces in 1913 to form one of the state's most successful co-ops, the Grangers Company Warehouse. The first warehouse was established at Covington, but by 1920, despite stringent opposition by local businessmen, Grangers Warehouse had relocated to Kent. Eventually the warehouse occupied the buildings now known as the Burdic Feed Company on Smith Street, where many older Kent residents remember the conviviality of conversations around the oil drum stove amidst a bewildering array of groceries, hardware, farm equipment, dry goods, shoes, feed, tires, and auto supplies.

The promising first decade of the new century witnessed a dramatic rise in the population of King County. During the same decade, Kent's population climbed no less dramatically from a low of 755 citizens in 1900, fully 100 fewer than the banner year of 1890. By 1910, the number had more than doubled to just over 1,900.

Many of the newcomers were first-generation immigrants from Europe. Italian and Swiss joined the Irish, Germans, and English in farming on the valley floor. Swedes, Finns, and Norwegians cleared the land and established dairies on East Hill. Here they put up sturdy and distinctive farmhouses built by Scandinavian carpenters Pete Englund and Magnus Peterson. Many participated in grange activities and the formation of cooperatives.

The largest influx of immigrants to the White River Valley came from Japan. Just before the turn of the century, young Japanese bachelors began to arrive on the scene, intent upon making their fortune and returning with it to Japan. Most worked first as wage earners on the railroads or in the sawmills and canneries of the new land. Others found employment as low-paid domestic help. Still others, born to farming, gravitated to the agricultural districts where they hired out as farmhands digging potatoes, cultivating berries, or milking cows. There was always work to be found clearing woods and draining marshlands for valley landholders eager to increase their productive acreage.

As soon as they were able the newcomers leased a bit of land, sometimes in partnership with a few of their countrymen, and began the operation of an independent dairy, berry farm, greenhouse, or market garden. Farming offered greater stability and potential for success than other wage earning work, and encouraged the lonely immigrant to send for his family or arrange for a picture bride from Japan.

Prohibited by law from naturalization and landownership, the Issei, or first-generation Japanese, were limited to leasing farmland from American citizens. Small tracts of five to fifteen acres were leased for around $40 per acre and rapidly converted to neat and efficient gardens. Husbands, wives, children, and elders worked diligently from dawn until dark in the fields, the average Japanese family netting no more than $1,500 per year. Season by season their number increased until by 1920, White River Japanese farms supplied half the fresh milk consumed in Seattle, and over 70 percent of the berries, fruits, and vegetables required by the major

FACING PAGE: Dr. Owen Taylor established this two-story hospital on the corner of Second Avenue and Titus Street to provide medical service to the people of Kent. The 15-room facility was headed by "Doc" Taylor and a staff of nurses who attended to births, deaths, accidents, and sickness until 1924 when a new, larger hospital was built in Auburn. Courtesy, White River Valley Historical Museum

BELOW: In the first 15 years of the twentieth century the village of Kent took shape as a town, ideally mapped out with tree-lined streets in quiet neighborhoods and farmhouse-style dwellings. John Nelson and his wife sat for this family photo in the parlor of their Kent home around 1910. The boldly patterned wallpaper and carpets, together with the lace curtains and potted plants, added a Victorian charm to this formal room used to entertain visitors and family on special occasions. Courtesy, White River Valley Historical Museum

cities of Washington.

The Issei were strangers in a strange land. While they struggled to assimilate through strong economic and social ties, many were determined at the same time to preserve their cultural identity. In the Kent area, Japanese farmers did business regularly with the local banks and growers' associations. Many branched out successfully into farm-related occupations in retailing, packing, and wholesaling. Some worked in the condensery,

tury that the village of Kent took shape as a town. From a commercial core astride the Northern Pacific right-of-way, blocks of sturdy frame dwellings fanned out to the east, west, north, and south. A regular rectangular street grid was established, although the north-south streets were slightly askew due to their alignment with the railroad.

despite the inevitable complaints about the taking of American jobs. Japanese children attended valley schools along with white children. When some disgruntled citizens sought to exclude them because they did not pay taxes, the Japanese community promptly agreed to contribute their fair share to the support of the schools. On Saturdays, Japanese children attended classes in their native language and customs at the Kent Japanese Language School in the old Taylor Schoolhouse north of town. Through various local churches there was some mingling of white and Japanese Christians on a social level.

On the whole, the Japanese immigrants were viewed with respect by the farmers, businesspeople, and educators who dealt with them. But others less tolerant were resentful of their successful inroads into the business, agriculture, and social fabric of the community. By the close of World War I, a strong anti-Japanese sentiment swept over the state, fueled by the narrow patriotism of the day. Kent area Japanese took part in the widespread Americanization movement, in an attempt to reverse the tide of ill-feeling by rapid cultural assimilation. Nonetheless, by 1921 the fervor of exclusionism culminated in the passage by the state legislature of the Alien Land Act, a racially biased law which would severely disrupt the lives of many Japanese Americans in the decades to come.

It was during the first 15 years of the new cen-

By 1910, the townsite of Kent was approximately one square mile in size, and the built-up portions of town extended roughly from James Street on the north to what is now 259th Street on the south, and from the Interurban right-of-way on the west, up the lower slope of East Hill on the east. In the residential neighborhoods, wooden sidewalks bordered quiet, tree-lined thoroughfares. The city commenced the paving of eight miles of graded, graveled streets in 1910.

Many new homes were constructed and older ones renovated in the real estate boom of the period. Neighborhoods built up before the depression of the 1890s consisted largely of one- and two-story, farmhouse-style dwellings with gabled or hipped roofs, and touches of decorative Victorian ornament. Porches, bay windows, and dormers were popular features. Not many of these remain, but the Ida Guiberson house on First South is a surviving example of that bygone era. In the early 1900s, the American Foursquare was a favored style. Generously proportioned and crowned with expansive hipped roofs, foursquares such as the Madison house on Madison Avenue North, the Irving Clark house on North Kennebeck, and the Ed Bereiter house on East Smith illustrate the growing prosperity of the business community.

With the development of the Knob Hill Addition, now known as Scenic Hill, Kent established its first exclusive neighborhood. Large, gracious homes, most of which survive today, sprang up along Scenic Way in the years prior to World War I. Many were designed in the ultramodern Craftsman mode, while others reflected period revival styles. All boasted polished landscaping and magnificent views of the pastoral valley and bustling town below. For citizens of Kent, a home on Knob Hill was the ultimate statement of success in the economy of the day.

Kent's business district experienced a wave of vigorous growth in the early 1900s. To promote the town and keep up with Auburn, forward-looking citizens pushed for the re-institution of a Board of Trade. Such a group was formed, and in the pre-war years community boosterism reached new heights. An outside journalist raved with enthusiasm:

"White River Valley, Kent The Metropolis," is the stirring slogan adopted by the Kent Commercial Club as the commercial battle cry of their hustling, growing city. Seattle's lustiest Princess is Kent, by right of birth and location, and destined at no far distant day to become a vital part of that mighty metropolis.

By 1913, the Kent Commercial and Social Club was going strong, and had established standing committees for new industry, transportation, legislation, public improvement, finance, publicity, and entertainment and amusement.

As home building boomed, so too did the construction of new business blocks. In the year prior to April 1907, no less than seven brick commercial buildings went up in the business sector of town.

Others followed in the years leading up to the war. A number of buildings survive from that period today in a cohesive historic district on First Avenue between Gowe and Titus streets. Together they convey the tangible flavor of another place in time.

Important new businesses opened up in the commercial center of Kent during these decades, not the least of which was Dr. Owen Taylor's hospital at Second and Titus. The 15-room hospital was the valley's first and only such facility until Taylor-Lacey Hospital opened in Auburn in 1924.

In the hot dry summer of 1914, a disastrous fire swept through a portion of the business district in downtown Kent. Although it was the town's largest such catastrophe before or since, no one was injured and damage was fortunately limited to one block of old frame buildings on Railroad Avenue between Gowe and Titus. The Sherwood Hotel, the Kent Trading Company, and other small businesses were destroyed. A lack of water pressure for fighting the fire was blamed on low reservoirs and the high number of people sprinkling their lawns at the hour the fire broke out.

Industry flourished and accounted for Kent's healthy payroll. Besides the condensery and the Interurban, three sawmills contributed to this economic well-being. At the turn of the century, both a cigar factory and a wood-pipe factory were in operation, and during World War I, the Simplex Bed Factory produced bedsteads for the military. After the war Howard Manufacturing, builders of ladders and wooden ware, took over the Simplex Factory. In 1917, a fruit cannery opened—the small-scale beginnings of Libby, McNeill and Libby.

Despite the progressive spirit that energized the town in these decades, life in Kent was slow and friendly. Yet Kent never fell behind the times, especially in regard to its leisure pursuits. Churches, schools, and granges still provided the chief forum for socializing, but new forms of amusement appeared in fast succession. The Dream Theatre, "the handsomest little theatre in the Northwest," and the Kent Theatre on Meeker Street offered the latest in moving picture entertainment, complete with live piano accompaniment. A bowling alley opened up in a new building downtown. Men's social groups sponsored "smokers," boxing and wrestling matches held at Odd Fellows Hall. Auto touring rose to the fore and dance halls became popular motoring destinations.

With the passage of statewide prohibition in Washington in 1916, a new brand of illicit recreation emerged. Countryside stills proliferated, and at least one local bootlegger in town was infamous for the number of nocturnal visitors at his door. Homebrewing became a common domestic activity, and children often participated.

In those days, everyone knew everyone in Kent and their parents and grandparents as well. Newcomers were always just a bit suspect, particularly after population growth stabilized in the 1910s. Local news travelled rapidly through the streets of town, and was served up nightly with the evening meal. The telephone company employed but two operators, and the night shift rarely handled more than two calls. The police force remained small because there was very rarely much trouble in town. Officers kept rowdy youth in line simply by knowing their parents. In those decades of rapid change, it was person-to-person communication, mutual trust, and a sense of complete security that gave Kent its distinctive hometown character.

FACING PAGE: The Kent Theatre, located on Meeker Street, featured the exciting motion picture Chelsea 7750 *in this photo taken in 1915. Owned and operated by A.S. "Pete" Leeper, the theatre had a loud and lively piano accompaniment to the films. Leeper also owned the Dream Theatre on First Avenue in the Guiberson Block. Courtesy, Rae Reitan Collection*

BELOW: An advantage of small-town life for children was the availability of special pets and unique forms of transportation. Willard and Jim Hurt drove a goat cart to get around town in the 1920s. Courtesy, Robert Hurt Collection

In the 1920s the Northern Pacific Railroad maintained a farm in Kent to replenish supplies on its trains. Poultry, dairy products, and vegetables were provided at the scheduled stop. The farm was known as the home of the "Great Big Baked Potato." Courtesy, White River Valley Historical Museum

Harvesting the Gifts of the Land

The agriculture of the Green River Valley reached full flower in the 1920s and 1930s. During these decades, Kent attained national prominence as a food growing, processing, and shipping center. Civic and cultural improvements nurtured in the progressive pre-war years came to fruition in the prosperity of the 1920s. But the same era was a time of upheaval and struggle for Kent's Japanese community and for all those whose lives were impacted by the Great Depression.

Although dairying declined in the valley's economy after World War I, it by no means disappeared. Among the prominent new dairy businesses of that period was Smith Brothers Dairy, which bought up the substantial acreage of the Standard Dairy on the West Valley Highway in 1930. Smith Brothers Dairy remains even today the largest producer in the valley.

Kent area dairymen increasingly sold direct to the Seattle fresh milk market through the Seattle Milk Shippers Association. The association operated its own loading dock on the Interurban line, and later shipped by truck. Some farmers, however, continued to sell to local processors, including the Red Rock Creamery at Kent which, in the late 1920s, produced tons of butter and cottage cheese (Red Rock Cheese) daily. In 1928, Red Rock was taken over by Kraft and a new plant operated by the Kraft Phenix Cheese Corporation opened its doors in Kent. By 1937, the factory gave employment to 18 local citizens and boasted an annual payroll of $30,000.

A new form of agriculture caught hold in the Green River Valley after World War I—poultry raising. The industry began as early as 1907 at the Ponssen Brothers' Kent Poultry Farm at the south end of Kent on the East Valley Road. The intriguing old Ponssen House remains standing today, but there is no trace of its once-extensive complex of brooder houses, laying barns, and incubators.

In the 1920s the demand for eggs increased to bring, for a time, a whopping dollar a dozen wholesale. The Kent Commercial Club's literature proclaimed:

The world famous Tancred strain leghorns are bred, hatched and raised one mile from Kent. Many farms of from 200 to 8000 hens are located near Kent. The vigorous fowls raised near Kent are sold and shipped for breeding purposes to every country on the face of the globe. One chicken farm, close to Kent, and managed by a woman, received orders for over twenty-two thousand dollars worth of baby chicks during January and February of 1924. Mild climate keeps the vigorous hens producing eggs, and the two metropolitan cities within 15 miles make an ever ready market for eggs and table fowls. It is estimated that there are over 200,000 chickens in the vicinity of Kent.

Built in 1927 on East Valley Road, the Kent Hatchery was only recently demolished. In one banner year, this business shipped 527,000 "skookum" chicks, and eventually took on the name Skookum Chix Hatcheries. The operation consolidated in 1937 with the Washington Cooperative Chicken Association, an organization designed to provide poultrymen with high-quality baby chicks at actual production cost.

The valley's poultry industry attracted experienced Japanese farmers who are credited with first introducing at Kent a technique for the sexing of chicks. The business flourished well into the 1930s until the stock became vulnerable to disease, and then went into gradual decline.

It was truck farming which overshadowed all other forms of local agriculture in the 1920s and 1930s. Several factors were responsible for its phenomenal success. Technological advances in production, storage, and shipping coincided with an expanding demand for fresh produce across the nation. Four transcontinental railroads operated through the valley in those decades, providing

direct access to eastern urban markets. Sawmills multiplied in the 1920s as farmers rushed to expand their acreage by clearing every last remnant of wooded bottomland. Last but certainly not least, the skill and thrift of Japanese, Filipino, and Italian farmers who leased and intensely cultivated small tracts of land contributed to the rise of commercial gardening.

Each with its peak period of ascendancy, vegetables of prizewinning quality and size spread the fame of the fertile valley far beyond regional boundaries—lettuce, cabbage, radishes, carrots, beets, green beans, asparagus, peas, corn, cauliflower, onions, rhubarb, and cucumbers vied for top billing. At the geographic center of the valley, Kent became the focal point for packing and processing activity, with associated ice plants, box factories, trucking firms, and cold storage facilities. Kent thus entered the industrial age, not surprisingly, through the bounty of its surrounding farmlands. Never had the pocketbooks of its citizens been so directly impacted by the seasonal fortunes of valley farmers.

By the mid-1920s, the production of head lettuce reigned supreme. For a while, the retail price of Kent lettuce amounted to over $2 million annually. No less than six vast packing houses sprang up at the north end of town between the major railroad rights-of-way. Here California dealers mingled with scores of local employees who sorted, trimmed, and crated lettuce for packing on iced boxcars. In peak season, 30 to 40 cars each

ABOVE: In 1928 workers readied chicks for shipment under the watchful eye of Ernie Engstrom, manager of the Kent Hatchery, located on South Central Avenue. Later called the "Skookum Chix Hatcheries," the successful business continued into the 1950s. Courtesy, White River Valley Historical Museum

FACING PAGE: Cleanly attired women graded string beans in 1937 at the Libby, McNeill and Libby cannery in Kent. Begun in 1917, the plant first preserved berries in jams and jelly and then turned to canning vegetables. Libby left the valley in the 1960s due to the growth of population and industry in the area. Courtesy, White River Valley Historical Museum

week left the Kent lettuce sheds for points east. Before the advent of refrigeration, preservation was the industry's number one problem. Many a boxcar reached Chicago, only to be dumped because its contents had become slimy. Valley farmers had to absorb the loss.

Much of the produce grown in the rich valley soil was processed right in Kent at the huge Libby, McNeill and Libby canning and preserving factory. The enterprise began modestly in 1917 as Kent's first fruit and berry cannery, turning out top quality jams, preserves, and jellies. It quickly expanded its repertoire to include pickles, sauerkraut, and string beans. The Libby's plant soon grew to cover three acres of land. In the late 1920s the firm had an annual payroll of $125,000, employing 130 people in the slack season, and 400 to 500 during the harvest peak.

In 1937, at the height of the Depression, Libby's placed an upbeat advertisement (using the antiquated "White" River Valley) in the *Kent News-Journal*:

On Libby's
20th Anniversary
in White River Valley
A SALUTE
TO KENT COMMUNITY

. . . These products from the garden spot of the Northwest, packed in the can bearing the famous Libby label, are shipped to the far corners of the earth. They can be found alike in London or Tokyo. This universal distribution brings back hundreds of thousands of dollars annually to White River Valley farmers! In addition Libby employs two hundred and fifty people in their Kent

cannery . . . So with pardonable pride they offer a salute to Kent community, with the hope that the far-famed produce of the White River Valley will continue to bring prosperity to Kent and the surrounding areas.

In the late 1930s, refrigeration opened new opportunities for Kent's food processing industry. F.H. Hogue Company Frosted Foods, Washington Frosted Foods, and Stokely Van Camp Frozen Foods opened plants at Kent in quick succession. Local trucking firms acquired refrigerated trucks, and a community refrigerator "Club Cold Storage" offered local homemakers demonstrations in the

preparation, keeping, and use of frozen fruits and vegetables.

As its industrial base broadened, Kent turned to enhancing the quality of its cultural and civic life. The Kent Public School system had always been a matter of particular pride to the community. By 1920, schools within the town itself included the old Valley School, reconstructed in 1903 after a disastrous fire; the Bowen School, a six-room frame elementary on the East Valley Road; and the "high school," built in 1908 on lower East Hill to handle the overflow from the Valley School. North and south of town and up on the plateau were scattered country elementary schools. From 1914, teens on East Hill attended the new Meridian Union High School.

In 1928 voters passed a $110,000 bond issue for a big new brick high school on East Valley Highway, or Central Avenue, at the site of the Bowen School. Its first phase of construction provided 11 classrooms, an auditorium, and a gym. The old high school then became Kent's first junior high school. In 1939, the pride of the Kent School District was its $144,000 WPA-built elementary at Fourth and Titus. No one was quite sure, however, about its stark Depression-era Art Moderne style.

District Superintendent L.C. Wright, who served through the 1920s, is remembered for the special emphasis he placed on the study of music. It was he who encouraged excellence in the high school's orchestra program, the beginnings of a long tradition in the Kent Public Schools. Close parent involvement in the schools began with the formation of the PTA, under Wright's administration,

RIGHT: Kent women rode in a "Preparedness Parade" in Seattle near the end of World War I. As members of the Red Cross, they aided the war efforts by sewing nightshirts and participating in other worthwhile projects. Courtesy, Marian Bigley Collection

FACING PAGE, TOP: Schoolwagons, depicted in front of Berlin Brothers store on the corner of Meeker Street and Railroad Avenue in 1915, were considered to be one of the first school transportation systems in Washington. The vehicles provided a safe and dry way for farm children to get to school. Courtesy, White River Valley Historical Museum

FACING PAGE, BOTTOM: Kent High School's championship football team of 1932 won all their games under the direction of Head Coach Claude French, depicted at right. The Kent School District field used today is named French Field after this legendary coach. Courtesy, White River Valley Historical Museum

in 1923. Japanese parents formed their own PTA so that they could fully participate, despite the language barrier.

Kent may have been the earliest district in the state to offer public school transportation. Whether by haywagons with hot brick footwarmers, or covered flatbed trucks with crude wooden benches, Kent's children were guaranteed a ride to school. Some were even lucky enough to ride the Interurban with their fare paid by the school district.

For Kent, and many towns like Kent, the 1910s through the 1930s were a golden age of community clubs—groups formed to push for civic improvements, provide cultural enrichment, and accomplish philanthropic goals. The women of Kent were particularly successful in these endeavors and managed to leave a lasting legacy of energy and commitment. The Women's Improvement Club of Kent got its start in the 1910s while working to obtain a local option law. After succeeding in that they remained together as a sort of umbrella organization sponsoring an array of projects and programs.

In its early years, the Improvement Club focused on city clean-ups and park maintenance. In 1911 they formally organized the Kent Garden Club to promote the beautification of town through the planting of trees and flowers. The Kent Music Study Club, also under the wing of the larger organization, took shape in the fall of

1926. They sponsored local choral groups, musical events, and originated the celebration of "Music Week" which later took hold on a national scale.

Kent owes its library system as well to the foresight and dedication of women. The Kent Free Library was organized in the spring of 1921 with an all-woman board. One of its primary goals was to reduce the loitering of youth in the streets. Temporarily, the library was housed in Kent's first Community Center, a converted old post office on First Avenue, but soon it moved into the new city hall. By 1930, the library proudly offered 3,200 volumes and 30 periodicals for circulation.

The men of Kent banded together for socialization in fraternal organizations, as well as for civic betterment through such groups as the Commercial Club and the Men's Civic Club. Local chapters of Kiwanis and Lions Club were formed in the 1930s. Veterans of World War I became active in Kent Post, No. 15 of the American Legion, while others joined the local National Guard unit and drilled in the armory on Second and Titus. News readers could follow the activities of the Guard in their weekly column in the *Kent Advertiser-Journal.*

As the town's population steadily expanded, Kent city government sought to keep pace, and several local officials made names for themselves. A new brick municipal building, designed by Kent's own City Engineer A.S. Leeper, went up on Second and Gowe in 1922. It housed city offices, library, and fire station under one roof. The new city hall was quite a feather-in-the-cap for the ad-

ABOVE: *High school plays were part of the early cultural arts offered in Kent. This 1925 play was held in the large Odd Fellows Hall on Meeker Street. This was the site of plays, musical events, and graduation ceremonies until 1929, when it was damaged by fire. Courtesy, Rae Reitan Collection*

FACING PAGE: *In 1922 the National Guard was well represented in Kent by the 148th Field Artillery, led by Captain R.E. Wooden. The unit drilled in the armory on Second Avenue and Titus Street. By 1929 the Kent post had changed from a mounted unit to a more modern, motorized unit. Courtesy, White River Valley Historical Museum*

ministration of conservative Mayor David Leppert.

In the 1920s and 1930s, the sleepy peace of Kent's streets was shaken. The inimitable Marion Imhoff served for the better part of this period as chief of police. Bootlegging kept Imhoff and his men busy in the 1920s, and during the Depression armed robberies in town rose significantly. Not infrequently, Imhoff discovered burglaries in progress in downtown Kent, and once faced a spray of accompanying machine gun fire. Imhoff gained fame in particular for one dramatic high-speed chase over dark country roads, the result of which was the arrest of a band of nine outlaws found responsible for more than 100 robberies in King County.

Improvements to Kent's municipal water system just barely kept up with the increasing demand, prodded by the visionary thinking of one city official, Irving Clark. Grandson of a Kent pioneer, Clark had served as city clerk and was acting as Kent's consulting engineer in 1930 and 1931 when he recommended that the city acquire water rights to Rock Creek Spring at Lake Sawyer, and land for a watershed around it. The city council could not envision Kent ever growing that large, so Clark acquired the water rights himself and later transferred them to the city. It was not until 1956 that the city acquired the Lake Sawyer acreage, by then at a much increased cost.

For the Kent Fire Department, the era of the hand-pulled hose cart and the horse-drawn hook and ladder cart ended in 1918, with the purchase of a new Maxwell hose truck. A period of true professionalism began in 1924 with the appointment of Charles Bridges as fire chief. During his 40 years of service in that capacity, the department acquired two modern pump trucks in 1925 and 1936. But most importantly, Bridges trained and drilled his force of volunteers to military perfection. By the late 1930s, the fire chief had 14 crack firefighters on call.

Kent lost a major transportation amenity and local industry in 1929 with the closure of the Interurban Railroad and its carshops. But at the same time, Kent stepped into the future with the opening of an airfield south of town. The Kent Flying Service, established in 1928, built a hangar with funds from the Commercial Club and bought a "Waco 10" airplane. The fledgling business brought passenger and mail service to Kent's doorstep.

Historian Clarence Bagley best summed up the progress of the community when he mused in 1929:

Today, Kent, like Auburn, has become a city that would amaze the pioneers who first started the straggling village of the '70s and '80s, could they behold its substantial buildings, its well paved streets, its park and band stand, and many handsome residences. With a population of more than 4,000 . . . Kent is one of the most rapidly growing communities in Washington.

Even as the community prospered culturally and economically, Japanese Americans in the valley faced a growing burden of discrimination. The Alien Land Act of 1921 dashed the hopes of many a Japanese family who dreamed of owning

age, and knowing no other way of life, sought to sidestep the spirit of the law in order to maintain a hold on their farms. A good many Kent area citizens assisted their Japanese friends or tenants in doing so by holding their lands in trust, eventually re-selling to American-born Nisei over the age of 21. Others like Frank Terrace and Shintaro Nakatsuka went to court to challenge the law. In 1926, a Japanese graduate researcher at the University of Washington assessed the situation as such:

Not even such drastic measures as these can kill a man's desire to live, to pursue happiness, and to feed

and remaining upon the land. The law prohibited aliens from leasing land anew and from renewing old leases, and made more difficult the possibility of Nisei, or second-generation ownership. American citizens who aided or abetted Japanese farmers by holding title in their stead, and Nisei who held title but allowed their parents to profit from the land, were subject to prosecution. Violations of the law resulted in confiscation of a farmer's land by the state.

As their leases expired through the 1920s, many Japanese were forced off the land and into new occupations. Others facing the onset of old

his family with the fruits of his labor. American land owners prefer to rent their land to Japanese because they pay high rent and take good care of the property, while Japanese desire to stay on the land because farming is their natural calling.

Though prosecutions occurred frequently in King County, and many immigrants lost their farms, others managed to survive through various manipulations of the statute. The federal Immigration Law of 1924 struck yet another blow by ending any further immigration of aliens ineligible for citizenship. Nonetheless, as families grew and

their contribution to the farming economy continued apace, the presence of the Japanese in the Green River Valley remained strong through the 1930s.

Anti-Asian sentiment or exclusionism simmered sometimes below the surface, sometimes overtly. Often it extended to include the more recently-arrived Filipino immigrants who worked as farm laborers. Both were subjected at times to ugly racial slurs.

The Ku Klux Klan was active in the valley in the 1920s. In March 1923, a representative of the KKK visited Kent and delivered an address at Odd Fellows Hall defending the Klan's policy of secrecy. The speaker was introduced by none other than Mayor David Leppert. Later that summer, the *Kent News-Journal* ran a front page article announcing the first annual "Konvention" of the state KKK to be held just outside Renton, with a nighttime gathering at Saar Cemetery two miles north of Kent, just off the East Valley Highway. "King Keagle" Major Powell defied the county sheriff to interfere. The event took place as scheduled on the night of July 14, 1923, complete with a fireworks display, fiery crosses, and 1,000 Klansmen, initiates, and spectators from as far away as Seattle and Tacoma. The crowd was "orderly" and no arrests were made.

To build solidarity and a sense of self-pride as much as to combat prejudice, local Nisei formed the White River Valley Civic League, a chapter of the Japanese American Citizens League (JACL), in the summer of 1930. In 1935, Kent hosted the large Northwest District convention of the JACL.

Buffered as it was by a fertile farm district, Kent weathered the Great Depression of the 1930s in rather good stead. There was never a shortage of milk or food; in fact, an excess of produce prevailed. Yet as prices plummeted, times

FACING PAGE, TOP: Stills, confiscated from bootlegging operations in the Kent area, were on display in 1930. Police Chief Marion Imhoff, second from left, and his men were kept busy during Prohibition and later during the Depression when the number of burglaries and armed robberies rose dramatically. Courtesy, White River Valley Historical Museum

FACING PAGE, BOTTOM: The Kent Fire Department's two engines were depicted beside City Hall in 1925. The front engine was a modern pumper truck and the second carried hoses and ladders. The improved equipment, along with better training of the firefighters under Chief Charles Bridges, helped to save many structures in Kent during this period. Courtesy, White River Valley Historical Museum

BELOW: During a spring flood around 1930 Dr. Hoffman paddled to his daily rounds near the intersection of Second and Meeker streets. The people of Kent, accustomed to yearly floods, kept rain gear and hip boots handy. New buildings constructed in the valley had high foundations to raise them above the floodwaters. Courtesy, White River Valley Historical Museum

were difficult for farmers, especially Japanese truck gardeners. This group formed cooperatives like the Kent Vegetable Growers Association, but ultimately the recession ended in their failure. Along with the regular influxes of seasonal workers and the occasional band of gypsies, the area witnessed a migration of Dust Bowl refugees from North and South Dakota, and an increase in the number of jobless transients.

In town, business held on by a slender thread, and some even flourished. Morrill's First National Bank of Kent was taken over by Peoples Bank and Trust Company of Seattle in July 1937, but the Kent National Bank survived as the only bank in the valley left intact. In 1936, when businessman John L. Fournier bought up and consolidated two existing Kent newspapers, he launched a 37-year family publishing empire with the first edition of the *Kent News-Journal*. Job seekers lined up in droves at

The three Becvar brothers of Kent (center, right, far right) established the Kent Flying Service in 1928. Together with Lloyd Armstrong, they secured a 53-acre landing field south of Kent and offered flying lessons over the surrounding territory. Courtesy, The Boeing Company Archives

the Libby, McNeill and Libby cannery with high hopes of earning a day's wage. Federal WPA programs provided some new jobs in town and in outlying areas. Kent, Panther Lake, and Meridian elementary schools were built with WPA labor, as was a new reservoir on East Hill and a section of the Bonneville power line right-of-way east of town. State Cannery #1, a community facility where families and charitable organizations could come and preserve their own fruits and vegetables, was WPA built and operated.

As they did across the nation, people in Kent found relief in extra doses of recreation. Clarence Shoff's Tackle Company, still in business today, manufactured fishing tackle during the Depression for a nationwide market of anglers. Townsfolk seemed to find added enjoyment in the outdoors, whether it was roller-skating on Meeker Street on Friday night, or picnicking at the shelter and wading pool in the park at Mill Creek. In private homes, people held "radio parties" complete with cake, coffee, and the usual radio breakdown. For more public

socializing, folks attended dances held in the big lettuce sheds, or motored to one of the many popular night spots such as Spanish Castle, Shadow Lake, or Lake Wilderness.

But the biggest extravaganza of all in the decade of the 1930s was the famous Kent Lettuce Festival. First sponsored in 1934 by the American Legion, the festival was conceived to showcase Kent, "Lettuce Capital of the Northwest," and was billed as the first of its kind in the state. In its brief blaze of glory, the celebration grew to attract over 25,000 participants. The inaugural Lettuce Festival of 1934 featured a grand parade, with first prize for the best float going to the Berlin Bros. store for a horn-of-plenty filled with lettuce. A close second went to the White River Packing Company, a Japanese-owned firm, for a great globe of lettuce with Kent as its capital. After the parade, decorated refrigerator cars of lettuce rolled in procession along the tracks through town, and 5,000 people helped devour the "world's largest salad." A lettuce queen and her court, which included six Japanese girls in traditional kimono, were crowned with great ceremony, and later in the day, the White River Japanese baseball team whipped the Kent Merchants team, 9-1. Beer and band music and dancing in the streets brought that first exhilarating, sky-blue June day to a close.

The festival spirit caught hold in Kent, and in the years to come expanded to include a soapbox derby, a visit by the governor, a Japanese fencing exhibition, and a grand fireworks display. The Lettuce Festival appears to have dissolved after 1937. The crop that year brought devastatingly low prices, and the spring of 1938 found Cannery Union workers locked in a bitter strike against Libby, McNeill and Libby and other local processors. But for those few short years in the depths of the Depression, the Kent Lettuce Festival drew together farmer and businessman, Japanese and Caucasian in a spirit of celebration, harmony, and hope for the future.

ABOVE: *Attired in formal gowns and kimonos, the 1935 Lettuce Festival royalty posed with Mayor R.E. Wooden (in military garb) and other festival officials. Queen Thelma Saito (center) wore the traditional crown and presided over festival activities, including a parade and ballgame. Courtesy, White River Valley Historical Museum*

LEFT: *In the late 1930s Kent Bakery sponsored this float, which was awarded first prize in the Kent Lettuce Festival. According to the festival theme, each float featured heads of lettuce incorporated into the design. In this case "Lettuce Grow With Kent" was a popular sentiment. Courtesy, White River Valley Historical Museum*

Sales of war bonds were an ongoing activity during World War II. Parked on a downtown Seattle street in November 1942, this trailer advertized the 6th War Loan to purchase B-29s and hospital trains. Speakers and a band accompanied the trailer and urged the populace to support the nation's war efforts by purchasing bonds. Courtesy, The Boeing Company Archives

Changes in the Wind

The future arrived abruptly in Kent with the advent of World War II. The global conflict forced rapid-fire change in the valley and served as a catalyst for its eventual economic transformation. In the postwar years of the late 1940s and 1950s, visionary projects of a regional scale began inexorably to alter the valley's established pattern of land-use. For some residents, a new era of opportunity had dawned, while for others, a way of life was ending.

Kent citizens' first local analysis of America's entry into the worldwide fray came under the *Kent News-Journal* headline of December 11, 1941:

Kent Mobilized, Unified in Preparation for Any War-Time Emergency; Nightly Black-Outs Emphasize Gravity of Situation in Northwest

Before the month was out, news of the formation of the Kent Defense Council, the kick-off of the Red Cross Fund Drive, and the sale of war bonds had reached every household in Kent. There was a prevailing assumption that the Pacific Northwest would be the target of Japanese attack. Blackouts and air raid procedures were taken most seriously.

In March 1942, the U.S. Army's Western Defense Command announced that pursuant to Executive Order 9066, all Japanese Americans, both citizens and aliens, were to be removed from Washington, Oregon, California, and Arizona and detained at camps on the interior. In the next few months, Kent's many Japanese residents were forced to register and prepare for relocation. Nisei landowners could either sell their property, or turn it over to a government board set up to "hold" assets of the evacuees. Valley growers were urged to step in and make arrangements to operate their farms for the duration. Some departing Japanese were able to store their personal belongings with local white families.

The dates of evacuation were set for May 8 through 11, 1942. Kent High School held early graduation ceremonies for its Japanese seniors, 24 out of a class of 92 students. On the appointed day, trucks were sent to the elementary schools to pick up the children. At Renton, entire families boarded trains for transport to the Pinedale Assembly Center near Fresno, California. From there, Green River Valley Japanese Americans were transferred to the Tule Lake Relocation Camp for two or more years of internment.

The uprooting of the valley's Japanese caused them incalculable hardship. Almost overnight, American-born citizens and their Issei parents, many of whom had made the valley their home for 30 or 40 years, were dispossessed of businesses, farms, and personal belongings. It is not surprising that many left with a taste of bitterness, never to return.

The departure of the Japanese resulted in a sudden shift in the valley's demographics. Shortly after evacuation, the government "redistributed" 108 farms, encompassing some 1,600 acres of land, to other operators. According to newspaper reports, local farmers reclaimed 60 percent of this acreage. Fully 40 percent went to non-residents, including Italian and Filipino immigrants.

Food production remained the valley's top wartime priority, but mass enlistments and the internment of many productive farmers precipitated an immediate shortage of field labor. Appeals were made each summer through the local paper to junior and senior high school students, women, local businessmen, and Seattle folks to help with the harvest. Early morning and weekend work was gladly accepted. To enlist the assistance of youth on the home front, the high school instituted classes in victory gardening and farm machinery maintenance.

The dearth of men in the valley also meant labor shortages in Kent's food processing plants. The canneries made seasonal pleas for workers. When Libby, McNeill and Libby blasted its plant

Women and men worked side by side to produce B-17s for the war effort at Boeing's Renton plant in 1942. The B-17 Flying Fortress was the foundation of the Army Air Corps' high-flying fleet. Boeing workers kept a steady flow of the bombers moving off the assembly line and into action. Courtesy, The Boeing Company Archives

whistle late at night, women from all over town came in to work a shift.

Local defense industry began recruiting female applicants as early as the spring of 1942. Kent's Northwest Metal Products Company, manufacturers of rifle clips, expanded in the war years to 240 employees. The firm soon won a much-publicized award, the "Army-Navy 'E' Pennant," for excellence in war production. Howard Manufacturing Company also recruited men over 16 and women over 18 for essential war jobs building parts for "Pacific Huts."

The area's greatest wartime employment opportunity was the Boeing Company's plant in Renton which offered high-paying jobs to one and all. Billboards and full-page newspaper ads carried the message:

Men and Women of Kent
Are Needed NOW to Help Build
BOEING FLYING FORTRESSES

. . . Your Government has stepped up Boeing production schedules calling for more Flying Fortresses . . . more women, as well as men, are needed now to do this vital work . . . high school students for summer employment . . . Special Bus Service Direct to Boeing Renton Plant from Kent . . . all types of work—in the production shops—in the offices—in the engineering departments...minimum monthly wage . . . $185 at the end of the 12th week.

As the war drew to a close, some organized resistance developed in the valley to the potential return of Japanese Americans. The "Remember Pearl Harbor League" circulated a petition to discourage their return, and many a community forum hotly debated the issue. In the end, only a small percentage chose to resettle in the valley.

The postwar years nonetheless witnessed growth in Kent's population. The "baby boom," as

Meeting on June 17, 1940, the Kent City Council sat for this formal portrait in the council chambers. Mayor R.E. Wooden, standing under the stars of the flag, presided over the city during the pre-war years. The council members included from left: Clarence Shoff; Harry Naden; Charles Sells; L.E. Price, clerk; Charles Bridges, fire chief; W. Falgren, engineer; R.E. Wooden, mayor; Irving Clark, engineer; Mons Rod, water superintendent; Dr. C.W. Hoffman, health officer; Emerson Thatcher, city attorney; Grant Dunbar; Oscar Barnes; and R.A. Thompson. Courtesy, White River Valley Historical Museum

well as increasing movement outward from congested urban areas, accounted for the expansion. A 1949 survey conducted by the Housing Authority of King County stated:

The mushroom like growth of the Kent area during the recent war years has brought with it the problem of providing housing, school facilities, and various public and private services for the residents of the community.

While the area within Kent city limits remained at one square mile, the population of the town proper expanded at a respectable pace. In the greater Kent area, however, the numbers soared more significantly. School enrollment in the Kent School District grew from about 2,000 children in 1940 to more than 4,700 in 1959, partly a result of district consolidation.

A profile of the school district's population some 10 years after the war suggests the kind of change the community was experiencing. Interestingly, out of a 1957 population of nearly 13,000, only 20 percent had lived all their lives in Kent. Twenty percent had moved out from Seattle, 13

percent came from other King County locations, and 9 percent (the fourth-largest segment) had migrated from the Great Plains states. Only 40 percent of the district's wage earners worked in Kent. Of the rest, a large majority commuted to Boeing in Renton or to industries in the south of Seattle. More than 85 percent of employed adults drove their cars to work.

This increasingly mobile, commuting population spurred a residential building boom in the outlying areas of Kent in the 1950s. No longer tied to businesses in town or to farms on the valley floor, a growing number of residents chose to build on hillside sites now easily accessible by automobile. Housing additions first sprouted up on the lower slopes of East Hill, then spread eastward on the plateau and opposite on the benchlands of West Hill.

In December 1946, the valley experienced yet another devastating flood of the Green River. Twelve thousand acres of farmland were inundated. Water flowed through the streets of Kent, and valley-wide damage was estimated at $1.35 million. The disaster encouraged the resumption of area flood control studies by the U.S. Army Corps of Engineers. Kent's community leaders and local organizations, the chamber of commerce prominent among them, pushed especially hard for Congressional approval of an $18-million scheme for a dam at Eagle Gorge on the upper Green. The project was authorized in 1947, with construction dollars forthcoming in 1955. Work on the massive public works project (soon renamed Howard Hanson Dam after its chief proponent, Colonel Howard Hanson) was well underway by the close of the decade.

The dam was widely heralded as a boon to agriculture, and valley farmers supported it en masse. But there were many—businessmen, developers, industrialists, and farmers alike—who from

ABOVE: *In 1933, flood waters inundated the town of Kent along Rail-road Avenue, Meeker, Gowe, and Titus streets. The Green River regularly overflowed its banks each year, and in December 1946 another devastating flood occurred, causing costly damage to homes, businesses, and farmland. Courtesy, White River Valley Historical Museum*

FACING PAGE: *Mount Rainier looms over acres of agricultural land in the White River Valley in the late 1940s. Open farmland existed north and south of town with housing extending up East Hill. The one-story Kent Elementary School, built by the WPA in 1938 on the Valley School site, lies near the middle of this photo. Courtesy, White River Valley Historical Museum*

RIGHT: *The Howard Hanson Dam, which was dedicated in 1963, stilled the flood waters of the Green River. By careful regulation of the river's flow, the Army Corps of Engineers was able to keep the Green under control throughout the year. This 1987 aerial photo illustrates the size of the earthen dam which, unlike many other dams in Washington, is not open for public use. Courtesy, United States Army Corps of Engineers*

Valley communities joined together through the Valley Cities Freeway Association to plan for a high-speed, limited-access roadway that would link Renton, Kent, and Auburn, with eventual connections to Seattle and Tacoma. The Kent Chamber of Commerce again played a lead role, taking a determined stand on the freeway's design, its route through the valley, and its funding. By 1957, the State Highway Department was committed to building the Valley Freeway, and its imminent construction was viewed as a given in the ongoing work of the King County Planning Commission.

With guaranteed flood control and a four-lane freeway in the immediate future, outside investors sat up and took notice of the Green River Valley. Large-scale land speculation exploded in the late 1950s. Corporations and railroads rapidly bought up acre after acre of farmland in anticipation of development perhaps 10 years hence. In the central valley, new landowners and local farmers intent upon selling turned to the City of Kent with immediate requests for annexation and rezoning to high-intensity uses.

Eager to expand its tax base and sphere of influence, the City of Kent moved forward. A rush

an early date perceived the broader implications of transforming a flood-prone valley into prime real estate. A promotional brochure put out by the Corps of Engineers made no bones about this potential benefit:

The Green-Duwamish River valley is also a natural area for industrial development . . . Freedom from flooding in the valley opens more than 10,000 acres of level land for homes, shopping centers, commercial enterprises, and both light and heavy industry. This means more economic growth which in turns means more employment and better communities in which to live.

A second important undertaking of regional significance hit the drawing boards in the 1950s.

. . . the discovery and development of the atomic bomb has brought with it an impetus for dispersion from congested urban centers of not only homes, but also businesses and industrial establishments.

The *Kent Report* classified Kent as an agricultural center, and recommended but three industrial locations for the city, one an 80-acre site on the north edge of town (prior to any annexations), another a considerably larger 2,860-acre site at Covington, and a third some distance away at Maple Valley. Of even greater concern to the county was the potential loss of local agricultural land to industrial expansion. The planning commission's 1957 *Duwamish Valley Study Area* report sounded a shrill note of alarm:

. . . the Green River Valley is the largest and most significant single area in King County which is devoted to agriculture . . . if all the proposed schemes for industrial development in the valley were carried to completion, there would be only 5,740 acres remaining in production . . . There is adequate and unused land in the county to accommodate industrial and residential growth without further smothering good farmland.

Clearly, the county's view of the valley's future contrasted sharply with the business, civic, and private property interests of many Kent citizens. The community was influenced by a long-standing tradition of reliance upon the value of the land. From logging to hop farming, from dairying to food processing, valley landowners had always willingly changed with the times. In late 1950s Kent, the

of annexations began in 1954 and peaked in the years between 1957 and 1960. The first expansion of the city limits took in the proposed housing subdivisions of Armcrest and Stonecrest above Scenic Hill. In 1955, an industrial annexation of 900 acres between the East Valley Road and the Northern Pacific right-of-way occurred. Another vast parcel extending west across the valley floor and up the hill to Midway brought in 1,100 acres. Finally, 2,990 acres of farmland north and west of Kent pushed the city limits all the way to Orillia. The city had spread from one square mile in 1953 to 12.7 square miles in 1960.

This phenomenal growth took place in the face of increasing concern on the part of King County about the placement of new industry. In the early 1950s, planning officials in Seattle and King County embraced the notion of "dispersed industry." The 1953 *Kent Report,* one of 14 area studies for a comprehensive plan prepared by the King County Planning Commission, outlined the theory:

RIGHT: Mayor Dave Mooney, an enthusiastic 23-year-old leader, took office in 1947 in time to help solve the problems of the post war building boom. During this period he also witnessed the development of the Kent Chamber of Commerce and the birth of a new community festival, Cornucopia Days. Courtesy, White River Valley Historical Museum

FACING PAGE: These two photos depict the corner of Meeker Street and First Avenue. The top photo, taken in 1914, features a Fourth of July parade. The Pacific Coast Condensed Milk Company, painted white, is seen through the welcoming arch on the right. The brick State Bank of Kent takes up the corner on the left. In the mid-1950s, bottom photo, the bank building remained and was renamed the National Bank of Washington. Across the street, Kent Hardware had replaced the Carnation Milk Plant. The telephone poles had disappeared from the scene as the utilities were placed underground. Courtesy, Rae Reitan Collection

prevailing sentiment was to expand the town's limits, or lose control of the economic future.

Although the valley buzzed with the excitement of a prosperous new tomorrow, Kent retained the ambience of a rural community through the 1950s. Agriculture continued as the most visible force in the local economy, and many believed strongly in its future. As late as 1964, the plant manager at Libby, McNeill and Libby avowed:

Farming in the Green River Valley has only scratched the surface and its future is as bright as ever, in spite of the inroads being made by industrial plants . . . Our shortage is in farmers, not in land.

But the old nemesis of distribution had become even more troublesome to valley growers—it was no longer profitable to ship local produce across country or even out of town. Big producers from California and Eastern Washington loomed as stiff competition. To the younger generation, fresh from military service or lucrative jobs in defense industries, farming no longer carried the same appeal. Perhaps the land would indeed prove more valuable for something else.

Kent municipal government in the postwar years flourished under the wing of Mayor Dave Mooney. Outspoken and controversial, Mooney was only 23 years old when he took office in 1947. But his administration soon faced larger and

more complex issues than any to date. Mooney welcomed change and the advantages he was certain it would bring. By formalizing the structure of city government on several levels, and by beginning the monumental task of expanding the community's infrastructure, he worked to prepare Kent for unprecedented growth ahead.

The 1940s and 1950s were the formative years of Kent's premier park and recreation program. A three-member park board had been established in 1930, but the real sparkplug for organized recreation was volunteer Pete Baffaro, who for years pulled together informal softball, golf, and basketball games. In 1949, the Kent Recreation Council provided a loose framework for these activities. Ten undeveloped acres on North Central Avenue were purchased by the city for Memorial Park in the early 1950s, and over the next decade the site took shape as Kent's first planned municipal park.

A turning point for the nascent parks program came in 1957 when, at the urging of community leaders, the Kent City Council and King County Commissioners agreed to jointly fund a position for a paid employee. Barney Wilson, now director

Formally attired and with diplomas in hand, the entire Kent High School graduating class of 1904 posed for this portrait at the end of their public school career. Included in the class were, from left: John Soule, Gertrude Morken, Eugenia Waite, May Haryward, and Bruce Bokyer. Most students of this era went to work on the farm or in business, with a small percentage attending college. Courtesy, White River Valley Historical Museum

Things have changed over the last 84 years for high school graduations in Kent, especially the size of the graduating class. The total number of 1988 graduates from Kent's three high schools—Kent-Meridian, Kentridge, and Kentwood—was more than 1,100. Of these graduates nearly 65 percent chose to pursue further schooling in a two- or four-year college. Seen here is the Kent-Meridian graduating class of 1988 participating in a misty outdoor graduation ceremony at French Field. Courtesy, Valley Daily News

of the Kent Parks and Recreation Department, was hired that year as a one-man staff. Wilson's first priority was to design a youth recreation program for a population on the verge of explosion.

During and immediately following World War II, Kent area public schools were reorganized through consolidations. In 1948, the Kent, Meridian, and Panther Lake school districts combined to form Kent School District #415. In the fall of that year, students from the old Meridian Union High School came down the hill to Kent. Community and parental friction over the consolidation was reflected in a spirit of fierce competition among students. Both student bodies sought to keep their traditional school colors and team names, so a happy compromise was effected with the choice of new colors, blue and white, and a new name, the Kent-Meridian Royals.

By 1959, the district employed 209 teachers and operated 23 buses. Enrollment had entered a period of rapid increase, and by the early 1960s one senior high school, two junior highs, and nine elementaries served the burgeoning student population. Kent citizens already had proven their now celebrated commitment to quality education for their children through repeated support of school levies and bond issues.

Kent entered a new era of self-awareness in

the years which followed the war. The town displayed a determination to aggressively plan for its future, to celebrate its present, and to reflect upon its past. Several key developments symbolized this newly emerging identity.

In 1946, the First Annual Kent Cornucopia Festival picked up where the Lettuce Festival of the 1930s had left off. As postwar prosperity spurred a building boom downtown, the Cornucopia harvest celebration drew thousands of participants and attracted regional attention. In 1948, the Kent Chamber of Commerce formally organized and began mapping strategies for the future at its board meetings in the Bungalow Restaurant. In the late 1950s, the realization of impending change inspired the first lunchtime gatherings of the White River Valley Historical Society. Clarence Shoff and Ed and Rae Reitan were among the families of Kent pioneers who began, along with history-minded citizens from Auburn, the important task of recording the fast-disappearing heritage of the valley.

In recent years the burgeoning expansion of businesses into the White River Valley has precipitated an ongoing residential building boom. Both single-family residences and multifamily complexes have rapidly taken over farmland, fields, and hillside lots. Courtesy, Valley Daily News

CHAPTER SEVEN

The Valley Transformed

Even the most prophetic of visionaries could not likely have predicted the profound change which has swept over the Green River Valley since 1960. As plans and schemes of the two previous decades came to fruition, the era of speculation wound down and industrialization shifted into high gear. The rampant growth brought on by this transformation forced Kent and other valley communities to leave behind their small-town ways, and, almost overnight, to seek urban solutions to urban dilemmas. Through the throes of physical and economic metamorphosis, Kent has struggled to reach a cultural maturity and to find self-identity. The many creative successes of the past 30 years suggest that Kent will continue with extraordinary resilience to meet the challenges of its second century.

The dedication of Howard Hanson Dam in May 1963 heralded the onset of industrial conversion. For the first time in history, development in the valley could proceed without risk of destruction by annual flood waters. As Colonel Hanson himself had predicted, "Old Man River, from Elliott Bay to Auburn, will be under control and the entire valley available for its highest and best uses."

Interstate 5 along the ridge of West Hill was completed in 1966, and Interstate 405, a ring around Seattle, in 1967. South from it pushed the long-anticipated Valley Freeway, which reached Kent in 1969. Up on West Hill just four miles from Kent, Seattle-Tacoma International Airport was expanded and modernized in the late 1960s. With air, rail, and regional highway systems now in place, Kent's prime central location enhanced its attractiveness to industrialists.

To its newly annexed lands, the City of Kent offered utility services that the county had been unable to provide. Assessments of $1,000 per acre were levied against property owners, farmers included. When Kent joined METRO in 1967, sewage treatment charges rose dramatically. The high cost of both water and sewage services squeezed canneries out of the valley by the close of the decade. With their local markets removed, fruit and vegetable growers already burdened with rising taxes felt lucky to sell out at skyrocketing prices. The pressure to develop increased.

The first large-scale industrial construction in the valley was a warehouse at Andover Park in Tukwila in 1961. Not until 1965, when the Boeing Company opened the Kent Aerospace Center in a pasture north of the heart of town, did Kent also enter the Space Age. "To help get man to the moon, we're bringing the moon to Kent," announced Boeing in a three-page spread in the *Kent News-Journal*'s Diamond Jubilee Edition of 1964.

Boeing Aerospace was Kent's first big new plant, and for a time it remained physically isolated in a sea of farmland. But other new developments soon filled in the fallow fields to the north, south, and west of town in quick succession. Tradewell Stores, Inc., arrived in 1965, Cam Industries and Northwest Steel Rolling Mills in 1966, Western Electric in 1967, and Tally Corporation in 1968. New industries continued to locate in Kent through the 1970s, creating a major industrial center of considerable scope and influence.

At first Kent's thriving industries generally fell into one of two categories—warehousing/distribution, or manufacturing. By the 1980s, however, high-tech electronic, computer, and aerospace firms predominated. Four out of five top employers in Kent in 1985/1986 were electronics-related businesses. The nature of Kent's industrial base is still in flux. Today's development includes growing numbers of service industries, offices, and retail operations. Kent continues to welcome new industry on acreage currently zoned and available for development.

As business boomed, waves of new employees and their families moved into Kent. Although the most sizeable annexations were com-

plete by 1960, the city limits have expanded steadily until they now encompass over 18 square miles. From 1960 to 1970, the population of the city proper grew from 9,000 to 17,700. By 1980, the number had reached 23,150. In this centennial year, 1990, Kent boasts a population of well over 35,000 and climbing. Even more astounding are population figures and projections for the Greater Kent area, including the rapidly developing Soos Creek Plateau to the east.

This dramatic growth soon made evident the crucial importance of a thoroughly modern, efficient city government. Kent operates under a mayor-council form of government with an appointed city administrator. Mayor Isabel Hogan, Kent's first female mayor, moved the administration into a fine new four-story brick city hall on Fourth and Gowe. When completed in 1971, the new building comfortably housed all city offices, including police headquarters, jail, courtroom, and council chambers.

The growing pains Kent experienced in its

In 1971 Kent celebrated the opening of the new city hall and library complex. Located on Fourth Avenue and Gowe Street, the city hall has four stories of offices, originally including the council chambers, police, courtroom, and jail. Completion of a new jail in 1986 and courthouse in 1988 along South Central Avenue made room for the expansion of office space at city hall. Courtesy, City of Kent

first decade of industrialization also underscored the need for professional land-use planning. Where would thousands of newcomers live, work, and play in the not-so-distant future? During the 1950s and 1960s, volunteers serving on the influential Kent Planning Commission sought to keep pace with ever-accelerating growth, but they were hampered by lack of a permanent staff. In 1969, Kent's first full-time planning director, James Harris, came on board. Today his department operates with a staff of 22, handling a full range of urban construction and land-use functions.

Harris's first task was to revise a zoning code by then thoroughly outmoded. Incrementally, the face of decision-making in Kent began to change as Harris pushed for citizen participation and policy planning. To stay philosophically ahead of the impacts of runaway growth, a new Comprehensive Plan was prepared and approved by the city council in January 1977. In its foreword, the new "comp plan" both sounded a warning and issued a challenge:

LEFT: Kent's official city crest features a fighting stallion and the Latin motto Invicta, *which means "unconquerable." Adopted by the city during the administration of Mayor Alex Thornton, the crest originated in the County of Kent, England. A familiar sight, the crest is displayed on all city vehicles and printed on all official correspondence. Courtesy, City of Kent*

BELOW: The Boeing Aerospace Center was constructed along the West Valley Highway in 1965. Boeing became the first major business to locate in the Kent area after the Howard Hanson Dam freed the valley from the floods of the Green River. The Boeing plant has expanded through the years with many new buildings added to the original site, and acquisitions of buildings across the highway. Courtesy, The Boeing Company Archives

1976 and the years ahead seem destined to bring still more change and hence more challenges to our self-determination . . . If the City does not take the lead in providing strong directions for the future, Kent will find itself unable to respond as a community to the outside influences which so greatly affect us . . . Hopefully by addressing the future thoughtfully and purposefully we can overcome the physical, cultural and governmental sprawl which threatens to absorb us. We can, if we choose, direct and control our growth.

Among the thorniest of problems encountered in this period of rapid change has been that of housing. In the 1960s and 1970s, residential development of single-family homes spread like wildfire on East and West Hills. Seven new community shopping centers designed to meet the demands of these burgeoning neighborhoods had

already opened by 1964. While Scenic Hill and other older residential sections in Kent remained intact, an increasingly large percentage of the population resided in planned developments some distance from the traditional town center. Multi-family housing units mushroomed after 1970 on East Hill and on the valley floor. By the late 1980s, people in Kent became concerned about the proliferation of apartment and condominium units. To stem the tide, the city council recently enacted a 20 percent reduction in density on multifamily-zoned lands.

Kent's strategic location in relation to a regional highway system has proven both a boon and a headache to residents and businesses alike. As a major employment center, it is estimated that Kent now experiences a daily influx of 40,000 workers and their automobiles. As a suburban bedroom community midway between Seattle and Tacoma, the city also sends forth thousands upon the freeways each day. The mounting traffic congestion which plagues Kent and other Puget Sound communities is recognized as an area where planning has been outpaced by the region's growth. In Kent, improvement work has recently begun on one of three east-west arterials designed to provide better access from the heavily populated residential areas east of town, across the valley floor to I-5. Kent is increasingly involved in regional transportation planning efforts, including study of a commuter rail service reminiscent of the old Interurban.

As the rural character of Kent bowed to the pressure of growth and development, its people launched a concerted effort to retain green open spaces for public enjoyment. Again the city played a leading role. With the strong support of Mayor

Hogan, the Kent Parks and Recreation Department under the direction of Barney Wilson emerged as an aggressive, award-winning program. The department began pushing to acquire undeveloped lands as early as 1965. Now the city boasts over 550 acres of parks and open spaces in a wide range of settings.

The jewel of the city park system is Mill Creek Canyon Earthworks Park, a lovely 100-acre wooded ravine where Peter Saar once operated his flourishing sawmill. At the base of the park are the intriguing earthwork sculptures of artist Herbert Bayer. Since its completion in 1982, the park has become a well-loved gathering place

The historic Neely-Soames house near Russell Road Park in Kent is now owned by the city. Donated by Ruby Neely Soames in 1985, the home sits by the Green River on part of the original David Neely Donation Land Claim of 1853. This image depicts the house and family in the 1890s. Courtesy, White River Valley Historical Museum

for the entire community, and a symbol of its liveability. Like Mill Creek Canyon Park, others in the Kent system take advantage of natural features: Lake Fenwick Park, Garrison Creek Park, and the Green River Corridor parks of Briscoe, Van Doren's Landing, and Russell Woods are among them.

Evolved from volunteer beginnings over 30

years ago, the city's recreation programs are second to none. Their strength stems in large part from a unique partnership of shared facilities and programs with the Kent School District. Kent Parks and Recreation now manages a 49,000-square-foot indoor sports facility at Kent Commons, an 18-hole, 72-par championship golf course at Riverbend, a Special Populations Resource Center, and an array of sports fields, tennis courts, and playgrounds.

Another way in which Kent has responded to the dilemma of its disappearing open space has been to directly face the issue of farmlands preservation. In 1982, the Planning Department conducted an Agricultural Lands Study which noted that since 1960, approximately 3,000 acres of prime agricultural soils had been converted to urban uses in Kent alone. The study further recommended that an agricultural zone be established where land-use would be limited to farming and related activities. Recently, the Kent City Council acted upon this recommendation by rezoning lands south and west of Green River, still largely untouched by urbanization, to agricultural. With this action, Kent has reversed the 30-year trend toward total attrition of farming in Kent, and given new encouragement to a century-old way of life in the valley.

The era of modern social services in Kent might be said to date from 1969, when the Valley Medical Center opened between Kent and Renton. Today it remains the largest and best-equipped medical center in south King County. Since that time, public and private organizations devoted to the well-being of Kent citizens (a growing number of whom are low-income) have proliferated. When reduced federal support in the 1980s threatened a funding crisis at the local level, Kent established the Human Services Commission. Annually, the commission assesses a wide range of community needs, from food, clothing, and family counseling to job training. Funding recommendations to local service-providers are made, as of January 1990, from the commission's one percent share of the city's general fund.

Mayor Dan Kelleher cut the first piece of centennial birthday cake at the official Kent Birthday Party on May 28, 1990. Held at Mill Creek Canyon Earthworks Park, the three-day Centennial Celebration ran from May 26 through May 28 and featured a food fair, arts and crafts booths, a historical walking tour, and entertainment. Courtesy, Valley Daily News

In the rush of progress, it might have been expected that the cultural vitality of the city would lag behind. It has not. On the contrary, by the 1980s Kent emerged as a regional leader in education and the arts. Both of these enjoy the strong support of the business community through the Kent Chamber of Commerce Foundation for the Arts and Education.

Even as the population exploded, top quality schools remained a high priority for Kent voters. Four public school districts now serve the greater Kent area—Kent, Renton, Highline, and Federal Way. The Kent District, which covers 73 square miles of central and eastern Kent, regularly garners awards for excellence in administration, teaching, and student achievement. Known for its commitment to a basic skills cur- riculum, the district also offers outstanding programs in science, music, drama and debate, and athletics.

Over the past 15 years, Kent has earned a reputation of solid, formal support for the arts. Both public and private arts organizations have contributed richly to the quality of life in the growing city. A local arts board was first conceived in the early 1970s when Mayor Hogan assembled a group of citizens to review the commissioning of artwork for the new city hall. Now administered by the

Kent Parks and Recreation Department, the Kent Arts Commission points proudly to a string of important successes. Their work officially began in 1976 with the funding of the first of Kent's downtown murals commemorating historic themes, the Carnation Company mural at Old City Hall Park. Among the commission's award-winning accomplishments of the last decade are support and funding for the earthworks sculpture at Mill Creek Park; sponsorship of popular concert series, symposiums, and festivals; and establishment of a per capita tax for art in public places. Present-day arts organizations in Kent range from the Rainier Symphony to the Evergreen Piece-Makers.

Historic preservation in Kent has taken a number of divergent directions since the founding of the White River Valley Historical Society and the first appointment by Mayor Hogan of an honorary city historian. Much of the area's turn-of-the-century building stock has been swallowed up by the pressure of development. The attrition of rural farmsteads has been particularly acute, but central Kent's older residential neighborhoods and its historic downtown district have by a happy stroke of luck remained remarkably intact.

Several significant historic buildings are under consideration for acquisition, restoration, and/or adaptive reuse by the city—the Burlington Northern Depot, built about 1924 for the Northern Pacific at the center of town; the pioneer David F. Neely farmhouse on Russell Road; and the Ponssen House, headquarters of the old poultry farm on South Central Avenue.

As it has across the country, the proliferation of new commercial centers all over the greater Kent area has tended to erode the economic health of downtown. The Kent Development Association, a nonprofit group of downtown merchants and property owners, began its energetic campaign to revitalize the old shopping district in the mid-1970s. Since that time, this group has worked to enliven the area with historic lighting, banners and planters, directional signing, and other street amenities. Known today as the Kent Downtown Association, the organization continues to promote the image of downtown as a unique people-place. To help guide permitting decisions in the downtown area, an inventory of historic commercial buildings has been recently expanded and updated. Under the current administration of Mayor Dan Kelleher, a downtown revitalization task force is studying innovative ways to encourage new business investment in the traditional heart of town.

In shaping its new image in the 1970s and 1980s, Kent has blossomed into a city of fairs, festivals, and special events. Every Saturday is market day from May to October in the streets of downtown Kent. Spearheaded by the Kent Development Association, the popular open-air market re-creates the spirit of early-day agricultural Kent, and draws pedestrians into downtown for weekend shopping. Saturday Market has expanded in its first 16 seasons from less than 30 to upwards of 100 participating vendors. Farm-grown produce, handicrafts and music, historic downtown walking tours, and lots of local color are just a few of its many attractions.

Cornucopia Days Street Fair and Festival is a three-day downtown event which has evolved from its postwar beginnings in the 1940s. The Children's Parade and Ezra Meeker Days were two subsequent versions. Sponsored by the Kent Lions Club, Cornucopia Days features street booths, entertainment, a carnival, and a grand parade. For old times' sake, in the centennial year of 1990 Cornucopia will be billed as the Kent Lettuce Festival.

Canterbury Faire is a relatively new summer event sponsored by Kent Parks and Recreation, the Kent Arts Commission, and the Kent Chamber Foundation. The festival is devoted to showcasing the pageantry of performing and visual arts. Each August, top-notch regional musicians, artists, and dramatists share their talents in this celebration of Kent's English heritage. A Renaissance Village, a Fine Crafts Marketplace, and an English Tea add to the excitement.

In this year, 1990, Kent celebrates its City Centennial with a big birthday bash, and embarks upon its second century as an incorporated community. From out of the past and into the future, Kent brings with it the strengths of hard experience. The foresight to embrace new opportunity, the capacity to creatively adapt, and the courage of self-analysis are traits which will continue to stand the community in good stead.

While accepting, and even welcoming, the inevitability of change and growth, Kent remains determined as ever to keep the city liveable. Many city leaders envision a focus in the coming years upon enhancing the viability and special character of historic downtown, improving traffic circulation and housing opportunities, increasing support for human services, and promoting Kent's image to the outside world. Surely that image must portray Kent as a place where people today care deeply about economic opportunity, about environmental quality, and about cultural diversity.

"The Kent Glow" is just one of the special events that takes place during the Kent International Balloon Classic. Each summer about 30 balloons, navigated by pilots from all over the U.S., ascend into the Washington skies during the two-day celebration. Photo by Garry Robbins

ABOVE: One of four parks in downtown Kent, Kaibara Park invites businesspeople and visitors in search of tranquility into its authentic Japanese landscaped grounds. Photo by Gary Greene

LEFT: Flowing languidly through the heavily wooded west end of Kent, the Green River attracts canoeists to its peaceful waters and cyclists and joggers to its adjacent interurban pathway. Photo by Gary Greene

RIGHT: Wintertime often brings fresh snows to transform the Kent landscape into a pristine still life. Photo by Harold and Loretta Vaughn

BELOW: Mill Creek Canyon Earthworks Park, a lovely 100-acre wooded ravine, inspires visitors with its circular earth-and-grass sculptures created by Herbert Bayer. Photo by Gary Greene

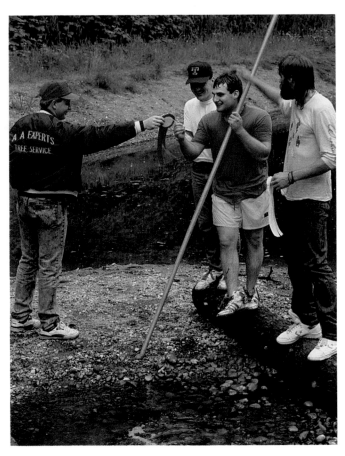

FOLLOWING PAGE: *Recently opened in 1989, the City of Kent River-bend Golf Complex features 18 holes of golf and a spectacular view of Mount Rainier. Photo by Gary Greene*

LEFT AND BELOW: *In May 1990 Kent threw a big birthday party at Earthworks Park celebrating the city's 100th year as an incorporated community. Included in the celebration was a logrolling contest, facepainting, and a variety of ethnic cuisines offered by local restaurants. Photos by Gary Greene*

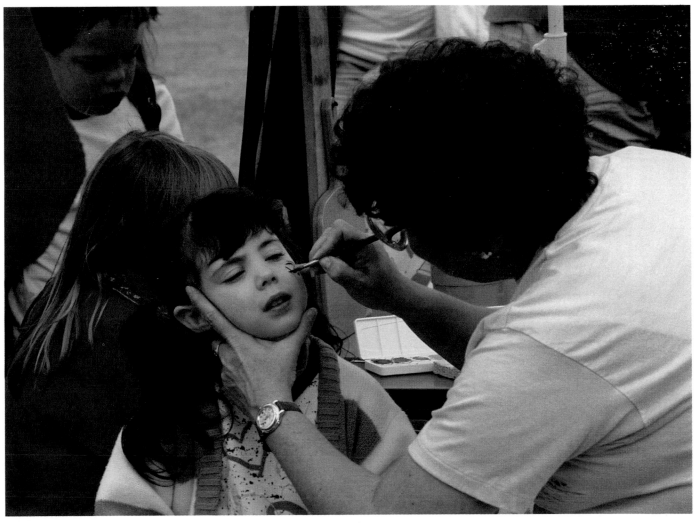

ABOVE: Cyclists or pedestrians moving along the Green River trail in Van Doran's Landing Park are greeted by "Slip Stream," stationary cyclists created by artist David Govedare. Photo by Gary Greene

TOP: Once a landmark in Old City Hall Park, the Carnation Milk mural was recently repainted at its original location, the Creamery building. A cityscape mural of Kent's Ukrainian sister city, Kherson, replaced the old Carnation mural, and old City Hall Park was appropriately renamed Kent-Kherson Peace Park. Photo by Gary Greene

With beanies, bow ties, and letter sweaters, the Kent High School marching band of 1925 posed at attention in front of the school on lower East Hill with the White River Valley in the background. The all-male ensemble kept up spirit at school events and football games. Courtesy, White River Valley Historical Museum

Partners in Progress

The story of Kent is the story of hard-working people who came with the dream of building a life in a community full of promise. Pioneer families found forested hills and rich soil perfectly suited to logging and farming. It was not long before the White River Valley was a belt of dairy farms, pasture land, and fields yielding hops, beans, lettuce, corn, and cabbage.

Construction of the Howard Hanson Dam in the early 1960s began economic change in the valley—a transformation from a rural community to an industrial center. With the assurance that farmland in the valley would no longer be subjected to regular flooding, more than 10,000 acres of land was opened up for construction of homes, shopping centers, commercial enterprises, and industrial development.

Construction of a freeway linking Renton, Kent, and Auburn with connections to Seattle and Tacoma provided further enticement for eager developers. When the city's utility services were extended to surrounding farmlands, many farmers could not afford the service charge and sold their land to developers. When the ports of Seattle and Tacoma were modernized and the Seattle/Tacoma International Airport was restructured, Kent proved an ideal area for industrial expansion. Warehouses, distribution centers, and manufacturing plants began spreading along the valley floor, transforming the pastoral landscape from agriculture to industry.

In 1965 the Boeing Company purchased 350 acres of prime farmland for its space simulation and environmental laboratories. As Boeing's demand for high-tech products increased, a number of companies were created to supply these products. In the past 25 years the lush, green valley floor has become a paved corridor of more than 2,700 businesses.

City leaders, service organizations, and concerned citizens worked to keep pace with the growing population. It has been through their vision and dedication that Kent now boasts an outstanding school district, 555 acres of parks, a state-of-the-art medical center, and plans for a new library. Strong support for the arts in the city can be seen with murals, statues, and sculptures, and Kent continues to preserve the friendliness of the past through its Saturday Market, Cornucopia Days Street Fair and Festival, and Canterbury Faire.

Sharing in the pride of Kent's history are its businesses. Those whose histories are told in this book have played a large part in shaping Kent's past and continue to influence its future. Along with their contributions to the town's economy, many of their business leaders have worked on preserving Kent's quality of life.

The organizations profiled on the following pages have chosen to support the preservation of Kent's history in this literary project and, in so doing, have chosen to support Kent's hope for the future.

KENT CHAMBER OF COMMERCE

If it had not been for the rugged persistence of Kent's chamber of commerce, merchants might still be pulling on hip boots to wade through flood waters twice a year. A new telephone system, public hospital, city hall, and a parks department are other major accomplishments of people whose visions became a reality through the Kent Chamber of Commerce.

Many of the early members of the chamber came from the Commercial Club, an organization begun in the 1930s to promote economic growth in Kent. In 1948 John L. Fournier, owner and publisher of the *Kent News Journal*, wrote a column about the need for a civic organization. In response to his urgings, the first meeting of the Kent Chamber of Commerce was held in February 1948. In April of that year, the following officers were installed: Orville E. Shoemaker, president; John Truckenbrodt, vice president; James B. Shiner, treasurer; and Tom S. Bailey, secretary.

The group worked to establish a thriving retail industry in the town that was sandwiched between Renton and Auburn. Renton was booming due to Boeing Company expansion, and Auburn boasted the Northern Pacific Railway terminal.

The chamber board met in the Bungalow Cafe on Meeker Street. In 1948 the chamber sponsored Kent Appreciation Days, which ran for 63 days and included drawings for prizes. The chamber also sponsored annual Christmas drawings, which were such a success that an Easter egg hunt followed.

The first large non-retail project was flood control. Members worked with the state, county, and federal offices along with civic leaders in Renton, Auburn, and Seattle in an effort to generate a plan for a dam. Finally representatives went to Washington, D.C., and convinced

the Army Corps of Engineers that the valley had flooding problems. With the help of Senator Warren Magneson, the Howard H. Hanson Dam was dedicated in May 1962.

The next big project was the establishment of a telephone system. Prior to 1960 Kent telephone users had to go through an operator to complete a call, but in that year the chamber was able to expedite a local telephone system.

After the telephone project, the chamber began working on a plan for construction of a freeway connecting Renton, Kent, and Auburn. The chamber also jumped into action to support the establishment of a hospital. After much negotiation with Renton officials, a site was selected between the two cities and Valley General Hospital was subsequently opened in November 1969.

As the chamber grew, there was a movement to establish a full-time chamber manager. When Harold Heath came aboard as president, he hired Tom Perkins after conducting a nationwide search for a manager.

In 1965 another chamber project resulted in the establishment of a parks department, and Barney Wilson was asked to serve as full-time

recreation director for the city. Since then, Wilson and the Kent Parks Department have set aside more than 530 acres for parks and recreational facilities. In 1988 the department was selected as the National Gold Medal winner for Parks and Recreation Management for cities with populations between 20,000 and 50,000.

Now with an area population of more than 100,000 people, Kent has moved to center stage in South King County's commercial and residential growth. As preparations for the twenty-first century unfold, the Kent Chamber of Commerce's attention is focused on leadership development, from Kent's youth to corporate boardrooms, in anticipation of a new era of growth management and regional cooperation. Kent's future will be as bright as the vision and strength of its leaders—leaders who can influence the city's quality of life, economic stability, trained work force, and global positioning.

(Left to right) Chris King, U.S. Bank, vice president/member services 1989-90, president-elect 1990-91; John Lindseth, Amway, chamber president 1989-90; Mark McKay, CASCO, president-elect 1989-90, president 1990-91; Suzette A. Cooke, Kent Chamber of Commerce executive director.

BOWEN SCARFF FORD-VOLVO, INC.

The name Scarff has been associated with Ford automobiles in the Green River Valley for three generations, beginning with Way Scarff, who opened his store in Auburn in 1922. Selling iron-wheel tractors and Model Ts, the elder Scarff established a tradition of public service based on integrity and strong, ethical business principles. Two of Way Scarff's sons, Robert and Cal, still operate the original Auburn dealership, Scarff Motors.

Bowen Scarff, the second of three sons, carried this tradition with him to Kent, and in 1958 opened his own Ford dealership. Located at the corner of Central and Smith, the first Bowen Scarff Ford operated with two salesmen and five mechanics on a 120 by 120 foot lot. The one-car showroom produced gross sales of $650,000 in its first year of operation.

The company rapidly outgrew the site known as the "Colorful Ford Corner," and in 1964 the operation was moved to its present location at 1157 North Central. Meeting the demands of growth, the company expanded rapidly, remodeled several times, acquired property to the south for a used-car operation, and built a body, paint, and truck center on the west side of Kent.

A strong community activist, Bowen Scarff has served as president of the Kent Rotary Club, the Kent Chamber of Commerce, and the Washington State Automobile Dealers' Association. He also served as a hospital commissioner from 1968 to 1973.

The acquisition of the Volvo franchise in 1984 has increased the company's parts and service business by one-third. A new showroom and office facility for the Volvo franchise was built just to the south of the main Ford showroom on North Central Avenue.

"Our goal always has been to build our sales based on repeat customers," Bowen says of his business that is known as "The Believable Ford Store." Crediting those who work in the business for its success, he emphasizes the high-quality performance of many longtime employees, such as Otto Speck, who recently retired after 32 years with the company. "Quality people can deliver quality service," Scarff maintains.

Employees of the company are proud to point out that their com-

Bowen Scarff

Bowen Scarff Ford-Volvo stands at the north entrance of the city of Kent. Photo by Aerolist Photographers Inc.

pany is one of 40 Ford dealerships in the entire country to be awarded the Ford Distinguished Dealer award for 25 consecutive years. The most treasured award a Ford or Lincoln-Mercury dealership can now receive is the President's Award, based on customer-satisfaction surveys sent directly by the factory to buyers of Fords. Only 120 dealerships out of 5,000 Ford and Lincoln-Mercury dealerships in the country win this award each year. Bowen Scarff has been the only dealership in three northwestern states to win the President's Award in three of the past five years. The company was also selected for the 1975 *Time* magazine Dealer of the Year award.

Bowen's eldest son Mike joined his father in the Ford business in 1982 after three years as a CPA with the firm of Price, Waterhouse. He is the general manager of the company. Son Mark also is working in the family business.

From 11 employees in 1958, Bowen Scarff Ford-Volvo has expanded to 106 employees who produce $50 million in annual sales and earn a payroll of $4 million.

Van Doren's Landing, the largest of the company's industrial parks, showcases bold new ideas in landscaping and design.

UNION PACIFIC REALTY COMPANY

Like many towns, Kent owes much of its growth to the history and presence of the railroad. The Union Pacific Realty Company continues that legacy through innovative development of formerly railroad-owned properties, including seven business parks in the Kent Valley worth more than $175 million.

The prime mover behind the success of the realty company has been Ted Knapp, director of real estate operations.

Formerly Upland Industries, a subsidiary of Union Pacific Corporation, Union Pacific Realty was organized in 1987 to develop Union Pacific's prime properties. Knapp joined Union Pacific in 1973, after graduating from the University of Nebraska. He came to Seattle in 1978 as assistant manager of Upland Industries and became director in 1983. In 1989 the company moved to a sleek building just south of the Boeing Space Center near the West Valley Highway.

During the 1960s and early 1970s Union Pacific purchased land adjacent to the railroad with the strategy of developing rail-served industrial parks. More than 1,200 acres were purchased in Kent, Tukwila, and Sumner.

Union Pacific Realty has devel-

oped seven parks in southern King County ranging in size from 30 acres to 650 acres. Along with the business-park development, Knapp and his staff of nine have been responsible for developing or disposing of other Union Pacific properties across the state. The company is redeveloping the historic Union Station in Seattle as the focal point of a phased million-square-foot office complex.

Largely because of Knapp's community involvement and the company's attention to environmental concerns, the largest landowner in the Kent Valley has escaped the negative connotations often attached to developers. Recently Knapp was selected as one of Kent's 10 outstanding community leaders, and the City of Kent designated May 7, 1986, as "Ted Knapp Day." He is active with the Kent Chamber of Commerce and serves on the executive committee of the Valley Area Transportation Alliance. Knapp is also a board member of the Kent Economic Development Board, the Seattle/King County Economic Development Council, and the National Association of Industrial and Office Parks. Other members of the company's staff are active in Kent's chamber and other local organizations and issues.

One of Knapp's goals for the Kent Valley is to transform what he calls its "big box or smokestack image," referring to the concentration of warehouses and manufactur-

ing in the area. These industrial centers have been a mainstay because of their proximity to railroads, Seattle-Tacoma International Airport, and the ports of Seattle and Tacoma.

Van Doren's Landing, the largest of the company's industrial parks, will do much to change this image with its landscaping requirements and design guidelines. Traditional warehousing functions on the 650-acre site will be hidden behind attractive office developments, restaurants, retail shops, the new Homecourt Hotel, and wide, tree-lined boulevards. Knapp expects 9,500 people will ultimately work in Van Doren's Landing.

"We constantly have to step back and look at the big picture, because our mark on the communities in which we develop is significant and long lasting," Knapp says.

Union Pacific Realty has donated 23 acres in its various parcels to the City of Kent for parks. Although he has found it somewhat challenging, Knapp is making progress with Kent officials to convert an abandoned sewage pond to a storm-water detention facility and wildlife reserve. It would enhance wildlife habitat opportunities in the area and provide a pleasing view for workers in office buildings nearby.

Quiet diplomacy and patience have the been key elements in the successful development of Union Pacific's properties. Attention to environmental issues, building design guidelines, landscaping standards, and architectural controls are beginning to pay off as the properties are developed. "I am looking forward to the end result, the finished project," Knapp says with a smile.

Ted Knapp (left) and his staff have developed seven beautiful and innovative business parks in southern Kent County.

CURRAN, KLEWENO AND JOHNSON

Along with offering sage legal advice since 1948, the founders of Curran, Kleweno and Johnson law firm have played a key role in Kent's growth and development.

It all started when Jim Curran graduated from law school in 1948 and was told that a lawyer in Kent by the name of Jim Kelleher was looking for a partner. After encountering a flood on his first visit, Curran tried again and soon joined forces to begin the law firm of Kelleher and Curran. The first office was located at First and Meeker streets in what is now the First Interstate Bank building. Kent was then a city of 3,000 people.

In 1956 Kelleher died suddenly, and Robert E. Ratcliffe joined the firm for a short period until Jim's brother, Pete Curran, came aboard in 1961. With the addition of Melvin L. Kleweno, Jr., in 1963 and Stephen L. Johnson in 1967, the partners have worked together to establish a law

firm that has grown dramatically in recent years.

Part of the law firm's success has been the leadership all four partners have played in the development of the City of Kent. A commitment to community service has been a hallmark of the firm since its beginning.

Jim's service as a Kent city councilman, as one of 15 elected Freeholders who rewrote the King County Charter, and in many other community and bar association roles established the firm's tradition of community service. Pete Curran chaired the committee that joined together the Renton and Kent areas to form the Valley Medical Center. He served as a member and chairman of the hospital board during its design, construction, and early years of operation. Mel Kleweno served as president of the Kent Chamber of Commerce and Kent Rotary Club. Steve Johnson was member and president of the Kent School Board, president of the Kent Kiwanis Club, and was selected by the Jaycees as one of Washington State's outstanding young men. He presently serves on the board of the Green River Community College Foundation.

With the addition of new

lawyers the firm has continued to contribute to the community, with members serving on the boards of Kent Chamber of Commerce, Children's Therapy Clinic, Kent Chamber Foundation, South King County Activities Center, King County Judicial Selection Committee, and the South King County Bar Association Board.

In 1964 the law firm completed construction of new offices located on Fourth Avenue across from Kent City Hall. During the mid-1980s, with the addition of Mark Davis as a partner, the firm planned and developed the Kent Professional Plaza. A business park at 555 West Smith Street, the Plaza houses the firm's new offices.

With the addition of Dave Hokit, Larry Schreiter, and Joe McKamey as partners, Curran, Kleweno and Johnson enters the 1990s as the largest law firm in South King County. The firm now employs a staff of 34 people, including seven partners and seven associates who practice in specialty areas of real estate, personal injury, business and corporate law, estate planning and probate, escrow, employment and discrimination law, family law, and trial and arbitration.

(Standing, left to right) Jane C. Rhodes, Thomas M. Kalenius, Larry R. Schreiter, Jennifer A. Ewers, C. Peter Curran, Gayle M. Harthcock, Joseph A. McKamey, and Douglas P. Becker. (Seated, left to right) Melvin L. Kleweno, Stephen L. Johnson, James P. Curran, Mark W. Davis, and David T. Hokit.

VALLEY DAILY NEWS

Like a play with changing sets and a multitude of colorful characters, early newspapers in Kent traded ownership every few years until 1935, the year John L. Fournier entered the scene. Under his direction, the *Daily News Journal* was founded and Fournier newspapers remained one of the largest family-owned newspapers until 1982, when it was purchased by the Donrey Media Group.

Washington was seven months from statehood in May 1889 when Beriah Brown, Jr., arrived in Kent with a small hand-powered newspaper press and a nose for news and produced the first edition of the *Kent Recorder.*

According to Don Crew's chronicle of newspaper history, *What's Gone On Here*, Brown's tenure with the *Kent Recorder* was measured in months. Brown sold the paper to Captain Howard B. Jeffries, a colorful character who, according to Crew, "kept his guns displayed in his office, ready for use in reception of whatever individual might take overly strong objection to one of his stinging editorials."

John L. Fournier is the founder of the Daily News Journal.

Jeffries changed the name of the newspaper to the *Advertiser*, and in 1890 he sold the paper to W.W. Corbett, who once again changed the paper's name, this time to the *White River Journal.*

On the masthead of the *White River Journal* Corbett proudly proclaimed his common-sense credo: "Published to do good and make money." One item from Corbett's journal reads, "There is a rumor that Mrs. Frank Leslie Wilde is about to separate from her husband. Willie is lazy and don't try to make a living."

Corbett sold his interest in the paper to partner A.T. Van de Vanter in 1893. At about the same time a competing newspaper, the *Kent Advertiser*, was established. Owned by Lester I. Walrath and A.D. Osborn (later Colonel John R. Risedorph bought out Osborn's interest), the *Advertiser* advocated Republican principles.

The upstart seven-month-old *Kent Advertiser* prospered and soon bought out the *White River Journal*. The first issue of the new consolidated newspaper, which publishers Walrath and Risedorph called the *White River Journal*, appeared on July 14, 1894.

Hard times forced the *White River Journal* into a stock company ownership in 1897, and between 1903 and 1908 the *White River Journal* changed hands four times. Timothy Brownhill, the fourth of these owners, announced the *Journal* would be independent in politics and changed the motto to "Aid the cause that lacks assistance; against the wrong that needs resistance, for the future in the distance, and the good that we can do."

In 1915 Risedorph reentered the Kent newspaper field and began a "new" *Kent Advertiser*. World War I was in full swing, and by 1917 there was an outpouring of patriotic fervor often translated into calls for conservation of resources for the war effort.

*Since the purchase of the **Valley Daily News** by Northwest Media Inc., Dick Ransom has served as general manager.*

Brownhill announced that as his "patriotic duty" he would try to consolidate Kent's two newspapers. Kent's population at the time was 2,300.

Competition appeared again in 1923 with the first edition of the *Kent Valley News*, published by Sam F. Collins. It was the *Valley News* that attracted John L. Fournier in 1935. He is credited as founder of the *Daily News Journal.*

Fournier and Barber negotiated the purchase of the *Advertiser-Journal*. The consolidation was to become the foundation upon which Fournier would build the enterprise that ranked as one of the largest family-owned newspaper operations until 1982, when the paper was purchased by the Donrey Media Group.

After purchasing the *Auburn Globe News* in 1946 and the *Renton Chronicle* in 1949, Fournier moved the Valley Publishing Co. and its flagship *Kent News-Journal* into a building erected by Plumber MacBoyker at 212 First Avenue South.

Fournier immediately set about establishing the newspaper as a leader in promoting community service projects. A Valley Publishing Ski School was established and ran successfully for 14 years. The *Record-Chronicle* and the *Kent News-Journal* combined forces to raise $6,240 for needed equipment for the new $9-million hospital built between the two cities. In 1980 Fournier Newspapers published a special 16-page section with color photographs of the dramatic eruption of Mount Saint Helens.

In 1958 Valley Publishing headquarters was bursting at the seams, and, with the assistance of an investment organization, a new building was erected at 704 West Meeker Street in Kent.

To keep pace with the rapid advancements in newspaper production, Fournier installed a 16-page Goss Suburban offset press in the new Kent plant. This was the first Suburban installation west of Denver and north of San Francisco, and the fourth of its kind in the United States. The press had the then-remarkable capacity of 12,500 16-page ready-for-delivery newspapers an hour.

Valley Publishing expanded again and a 40-page Goss Urbanite rotary offset press was installed. It was capable of turning out 72 pages, with eight pages in spot color, at 22,000 papers an hour.

In 1979 Fournier Newspapers became the first non-daily newspaper in the state to install a "scanner" which, using a laser beam, could read typewritten copy and convert it to newspaper type.

In October 1967 the *News-Journal* was judged the state's best non-daily newspaper in an annual contest sponsored by the Washington Newspaper Publishers Association. In 1970 the paper did a traffic-safety campaign that began as a salute to Washington State Highway Safety Week. It continued for two years. As a result of the campaign, in 1971 the newspapers won the national Alfred D. Sloan award for distinguished public service in highway safety. A second national award came in 1972 when the National Safety Council presented Fournier Newspapers its prestigious "Public Service Award."

The death of Fournier on September 19, 1972, at the age of 68, was a shock to the Greater Green River Valley community. Upon his death, his widow, Jean, became president of Valley Publishing Co. She appointed John L. Fournier, Jr., publisher of the *News-Journal* and *Auburn Globe News* and Charles Fournier associate publisher.

Ten days after Fournier's death, Jean picked up her late husband's column, "What's Going on Here" and wrote the Wednesday page-one feature for the next two years.

After more than 40 years of operation under the Fournier banner, the Fournier Newspapers and its employees have won 895 local, state, and national honors for journalistic excellence.

With daily production the burgeoning company exploded out of its building, and an eight-acre tract was purchased in southwest Kent. A handsome 48,000-square-foot building was erected on the land, bringing the *Daily News Journal* operation along with the Fournier Newspapers production facilities for the Kent, Renton, and Auburn newspapers under one roof. Cost of the new plant was estimated at $2.8 million.

After the purchase of Fournier Newspapers in 1982 by the Donrey Media Group, the three papers were combined under one name, the *Valley Daily News*. In 1988 the *Valley Daily News* topped other media group papers with awards for best front page, best spot news, and best circulation promotion. In late December 1989 Donrey sold the paper to Northwest Media Inc. of Bellevue. Dick Ransom, former production manager of Valley Newspapers under the Fournier family, was named general manager. Ransom was with the *Journal American* in Bellevue, also owned by Northwest Media Inc.

Fournier Newspapers production was united under one roof when this 48,000-square-foot building was constructed on an eight-acre tract of land in southwest Kent adjacent to the Green River.

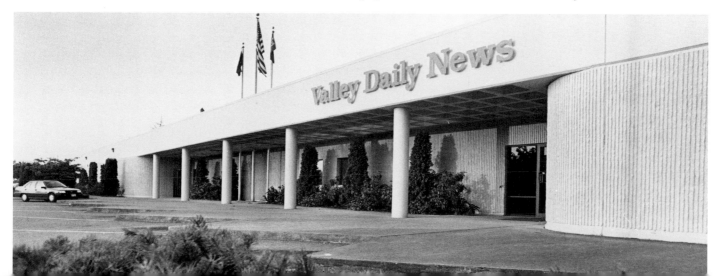

POZZI BROS. TRANSPORTATION INC.

In the early 1900s Kent's dairy and vegetable industry was booming, but transportation was limited. The Pozzi brothers, Chester ("Slim") and Jesse ("Bab"), saw the need, and in 1919 they began a trucking company that has retained family ownership for two generations.

The Pozzi Bros. picked up milk and vegetables from local farms for Seattle delivery. The trucks returned to Kent loaded with supplies and equipment needed by the rapidly growing farming industry.

The trucks lumbered over bumpy country roads to pick up milk cans left on roadside platforms built near each farm. Even floods did not stop the faithful pickup service, according to Tom Pozzi, present owner of Pozzi Bros. Transportation Inc. Amphibious vehicles, known as army ducks, were used to pick up milk and deliver supplies to flood-stranded farmers. "The army ducks looked like huge barges with wheels," Tom recalls.

Located in the heart of Kent in a brick building at 705 West Meeker, the company maintained two additional terminals in Tacoma and Seattle.

By the time their younger brother, Ralph, joined the company in the early 1940s, the Pozzi brothers had expanded the business to include general freight. Although 20 years younger than his brothers, Ralph Pozzi was a dynamic leader and a driving force in the company's growth. "He commanded respect wherever he went, and his contribution to the community was tremendous," says his son, Tom Pozzi.

Born in 1913, Ralph grew up on the family homestead at O'Brien, north of Kent. Early in his life, he exhibited leadership as student body president at Kent High School and later as president of his college fraternity at Washington State University. He served as president of the Kent

Rotary Club where he was a charter member, the Kent Chamber of Commerce, and the Washington Trucking Association. Pozzi served as a member of the Kent City Council and was a longtime commissioner for Fire Protection District 37. He was named Junior Chamber of Commerce Boss of the Year in 1963, and in 1965 the Kent Education Association awarded him Citizen of the Year.

After Pozzi's untimely death at the age of 53 in 1966, his son, Tom, was brought in as a partner in the business. Tom, who was 20 years old at the time, joined Slim Pozzi's son, Wayne, and Bab's two sons, Clint and Carl. (The three had taken over the company since their fathers' deaths in the 1950s.)

Tom had not planned on trucking as a career. "At the time of Dad's death, I was going to Seattle University to become a teacher and coach," Tom explains. While at college, he worked evenings and weekends driv-

Ralph Pozzi (second from left) and Bab Pozzi (right) pose in the 1930s with the owner of the dairy trucking outfit which they purchased and which has remained in the family for two generations.

ing trucks for the company—as he had done since he was 16 years old. In 1969 he started working full time with his cousins in the family business. Now Tom has sole ownership of the company.

In 1976 Pozzi Bros. purchased 4.2 acres north of Kent, and the three terminals in Seattle, Tacoma, and Kent were consolidated into one centralized location at 21441 76th Street South in Kent. Today Pozzi Bros. Transportation Inc. boasts 30 trucks, 80 trailers, and 40 employees. Although the original need for Pozzi Bros. no longer exists, the trucking company continues to haul general freight for clients in Kent along with those in communities throughout the state of Washington.

CITY BEVERAGES DISTRIBUTORS, INC.

Although Kent is no longer known for its hop-growing industry, City Beverages has taken up the slack as the area's major beer distributor. The company sells more than one million cases of beer each year, according to City Beverages president and founder, Ford Basel.

Only 100 cases of beer were sold in 1954, when Basel bought the beer and soda pop distributorship from the Cammarano Brothers. During those early years City Beverages flourished with one driver, one secretary, and Basel. Basel's wife, Iris, was the secretary. "She was my right-hand person," he says. "She did everything but drive the truck."

The company's first home was a 4,800-square-foot building located at 725 Saar Street. In 1975 a move was made to Third Avenue. In 1977 the company expanded when City Beverages merged with Valley Distributors. Fred Nelson, owner of Valley Distributors, became vice president of City Beverages Distributors, Inc., the surviving corporation.

Valley Distributors was originally owned by Nelson's father, Francis "Fuzzy" Nelson. The elder Nelson had worked at the White River Feed Co.,

selling beer and wine. Later he and a partner, "Slim" Thomas, joined forces, started Valley Distributors, and began selling beer and wine on their own. Thomas died in 1940 and Fuzzy Nelson bought out his interest. In the early 1970s Fred Nelson, who had worked in the company as a truck driver and in sales, ran the business after his father's death.

Nelson brought along four employees: Bill Wilson, Bill Mackie, Frank Junt, and Marge Selley. Another key player in the development of City Beverages is Ford Kiene, who now serves as the company's general manager. Kiene had worked for Basel during his high school years, delivering pop and washing trucks. He continued working for the company during college. He was selected as one of Green River Community College's outstanding alumni, and is a graduate of the University of Washington.

Kiene is active in the Kent Rotary Club and the Kent Chamber of Commerce, and is a past president of each. He is a member of the Kent Drinking Driver Task Force and a board member of the South King County Activity Center, which oper-

ates a workshop for developmentally disadvantaged people. He ran for mayor four years ago but lost to Dan Kelleher.

With its highly motivated team of managers, City Beverages plans on a banner year with a goal of selling one million cases of Anheuser-Busch, along with other beer products, including G. Heilman, Rainier, and Schmidt.

The company is now the third-largest distributor of Anheuser-Busch in the state and was awarded the gold medal in Anheuser-Busch's Dimension of Excellence Program. "The only wholesaler to ever achieve this level in the state of Washington," Basel says with pride.

After moving to First Avenue in Kent in 1979, the company built a 34,000-square-foot building at 1025 Sixth Avenue North in 1981. Now 48 employees strong, City Beverages Distributors, Inc., plans to continue its policy of hard work and service to the community.

City Beverages employees in front of the Kent office.

HEATH TECNA

The sleek interiors of one in four airplanes today are designed and produced at Heath Tecna's 800,000-square-foot plant on Eighty-Fourth Avenue South in Kent. Founded in 1950, the company prospered, struggled, and prospered again until it has become a leading supplier of high strength, lightweight composite structures and aircraft interior systems for the aerospace and defense industries.

Harold Heath was 27 years old when he started Heath Tecna as a machined products operation with three employees. At the outset the fledgling enterprise was dedicated to serving the burgeoning aerospace industry with needed manufactured parts. It was not long, however, before Heath quickly diversified the original enterprise to include both a plastics fabrication and a plating and finishing operation providing a unique combination of capabilities for the aerospace industry.

In 1956, with Boeing's expansion, the company moved from its original site on Eighth Street in Renton to its present site at 19819 Eighty-Fourth Avenue South. By 1957 the facility had tripled in size and business was booming.

In order to diversify and expand its product offerings, Heath Tecna acquired more then 17 companies

between 1957 and 1970. With $4,250 to start the company in 1950, Heath boasted a net worth of $9.5 million by April 1968. Sales from 1964 to 1968 nearly quintupled and earnings per share multiplied 7.7 times. Employment grew 345 percent.

During those years Harold Heath was active in the Kent Chamber of Commerce and helped fund a full-time chamber manager. Also, as part of Heath's community outreach, he spearheaded a program to employ unemployed people from the "skid-row" area of Seattle. Each day a bus was dispatched to pick up willing workers in an effort to help return them to a more productive life-style. In 1964 Heath encouraged the hiring of refugees from the Hungarian revolt to work at Heath Tecna.

Heath also was involved in funding a number of community projects, including the Saint James Day School and projects sponsored by the Kent Rotary Club. Heath asked William F. Kennelly, who was then senior vice president of quality control and personnel, to represent Heath Tecna on the Green River College Board of Trustees. Kennelly has continued to serve the college on a variety of projects since that time. "Whenever the community needed some help, we stepped in," Heath says.

By 1968 the company began expanding into other markets along with its subcontracting work for the Boeing Company. This led to Heath Tecna's participation in the fields of air-cargo and passenger-handling equipment and systems, nuclear and scientific products, and protective finishing. The aerospace group included three divisions: machined products, plating, and plastics. Art Davis ran the plating division and was a right-hand man to Heath in the development of the company. The founding operation of Heath Tecna was the machine products division, and it was primarily aerospace oriented due to its highly developed capabilities for volume production of close tolerance parts. These parts were made of aluminum, steel, titanium, magnesium, and other alloys. The customer roster at the time included Boeing, Lockheed, McDonnell-Douglas, Fairchild, Goodyear, and Aeronca.

In the plastics division, insulation for aircraft interiors was developed along with metal bonding, where resin cloth was used to produce molded parts. In its infancy, the plastics division produced a number of products, including Christmas tree stands, portable showers for campers, boat bumpers, molded doors for aircraft, and missile parts.

Contracts with Boeing for insulation were so successful that Boeing asked Heath Tecna to bid on other airplane parts, including the radome or nose of the airplane and wing-to-body fairings. The production of these structures led to the growth of the plastics division, which has become one of the world's largest pro-

Founded in 1950, Heath Tecna has become a leading supplier of high strength, lightweight composite structures and aircraft interior systems for the aerospace and defense industries. This photo shows the way the company's machine shop looked in 1956.

Heath Tecna's third plant in south Kent.

The business expanded to include a separate plating shop, shown here in 1958 when it was visited by Governor Al Rossellini (left).

ducers of reinforced fiberglass structures for commercial jet aircraft.

Plastic structures are cured in huge autoclaves constructed to withstand high temperatures. The first autoclave used at Heath Tecna measured eight feet in length and four feet in diameter. The company now uses six autoclaves, with the most recent one measuring 10 feet in diameter and 50 feet long.

In 1970 the bottom dropped out of the aerospace industry, and the company's plastics division suffered a severe blow. In 1970-1971 the company lost more than $13 million, debt reached almost $22 million, and the stock had a negative book value.

In 1971 Carroll M. Martenson, then a group vice president for Textron, was brought in as chief executive. The process was slow and painful, but Martenson pared things back to a profitable core and began moving ahead.

Larry Kring assumed leadership of Heath Tecna in July 1978, and by 1980 company profits were reflecting four years of record sales. Also in 1980 Heath Tecna Corp. became Criton Corporation, a name made up by a corporate-image consultant.

Today, with more autoclaves and advanced technological skills, composite structures for spacecraft,

missiles, submarines, and helicopters are designed and built at Heath Tecna. A few of these structures include interior sidewalls and ceilings, interior stowage bins, rudder panels, wing-to-body fairings, wing panels, and aircraft nose radomes. The company leads the country in building the largest deliverable composite structures used in the aircraft industry today.

By 1990 the company will have produced more than 2,400 interior systems for every major aircraft. In 1988 Heath Tecna Aerospace was pur-

Heath Tecna officials show off the new autoclave they purchased in 1965. The company now uses six of these machines which are utilized to cure plastics. This piece of equipment was 43 feet long, had an inner diameter of almost 16 feet, and was able to withstand over 450 degrees Fahrenheit and 100 pounds per square inch of pressure.

chased by Ciba-Geigy, a Swiss firm, headquartered in Ardsley, New York, with limited headquarters in Basel, Switzerland.

"Despite the changes in ownership, we are still Heath Tecna with the same technology, financial goals, and commitment to our surroundings," says Kring.

By 1991 Heath Tecna will employ more than 1,500 engineers and skilled workers who will design, develop, and fabricate advanced composite structures in a one-million-square-foot facility.

POE CONSTRUCTION, INC.

Fred Poe constructs buildings and community good will. As owner and president of Poe Construction, Inc., in Auburn, he has developed a successful construction business while serving his community in a variety of ways.

For 16 years, since buying out East Valley Construction, owned by Nap Hebert and Leonard Garneau, Poe has increased his company's annual volume from $500,000 in 1973 to $14 million in 1989.

Building his reputation on the simple idea of doing a good job for his customers, Poe's construction company has erected more than 140 buildings: warehouses, offices, clubhouses, stores, medical clinics, restaurants, banks, and truck terminals. Recently his firm completed the upscale Union Pacific Realty Building located in Kent's new Van Doren's Landing development. His largest project was a 240,000-square-foot distribution services building in Kent.

Starting with one office employee, Poe has steadily increased his staff with the increase in volume. Nine people work in the office in various capacities, and anywhere from 15 to 45 work in the field. At times Poe employs more than 50

people, including carpenters and laborers. Poe's son Charles works as a project manager in the business.

Poe's engineering background in school and on the job uniquely qualifies him as a leader in the construction field. He is a graduate in civil engineering with a BSCE from Washington State University and a MSCE from the University of Washington.

After graduating from college in 1956, Poe worked in consulting engineering for five years and later managed Smith Brothers Silica Sand Co. From 1966 to 1969 he served as city engineer and director of public works in Auburn. He then went to work for Leavitt Commercial Corp. and in 1971 moved to Dallas, Texas, where he managed the construction of motels and restaurants. In 1973 he moved back to Auburn and purchased East Valley Construction. Poe's knowledge of compiling detailed estimates and the company's expertise in concrete work, including concrete tilt-up buildings, put the company in a favorable position. It was not long before he was expanding the business.

Despite a busy schedule on the job, Poe has found time for community service. He was president of the Auburn Junior Chamber of Commerce, the Auburn Chamber of Commerce, the Auburn Kiwanis Club, and the South King County YMCA Board. He was an original board member

Fred W. Poe, president of Poe Construction, Inc.

and then president of the Auburn Area Economic Development Association, and served as a board member of the Seattle Chapter of the Associated General Contractors. He served on the board of directors of the Seattle King County Economic Development Council, and for the past six years he has been chairman of the Green River Community College Pro/Am Golf Tournament. He is the chairman of the Auburn Area Ducks Unlimited Chapter, and he is on the community board of the Sterling Savings Association.

With an eye to future growth, Poe is incorporating strategic planning and management training as goals for his company in the coming year. Using marketing expertise, he hopes to expand Poe Construction, Inc.'s options for building throughout the Puget Sound area.

Poe's construction company has erected more than 140 buildings, including the two-story office warehouse for Distributed Technologies.

IDDINGS INC.

Five generations of Iddings have worked the land for a living, and Jim Iddings is no exception. The great-great-grandson of pioneers James and Rebecca Iddings, who came west in 1875, Jim is carrying on the traditional family vocation in a slightly different form. His company, Iddings Inc., produces sand, gravel, bark, and topsoil.

It all started when his father, Earl, sold his dairy business in 1942 and began hauling wood shavings to farmers who used them for cattle bedding.

Earl started the dairy business in 1925. His dairy was located on 208th, more commonly known as the Old Wilson Road, named after his wife's father, Jim Wilson. Earl had a reputation for working hard, and, according to his son Jim, he sold the dairy after working 21 years without a single day off.

Jim remembers waking up one night when he was a young boy to the intense heat and glow of his father's barn burning to the ground. Flames engulfed the barn, a new milking machine, and bales of hay. "The neighbors all knew how hard

"We have hauled a lot of Kent soil from the valley floor to the East Hill over the years."

dad had worked to make that dairy a success, and before long they all pitched in and rebuilt the barn," Jim recalls. In 1942 an outbreak of undulant fever resulting from cows infected with Bangs disease led to his father's sale of the dairy and cattle.

In 1945 Earl began hauling wood shavings, and in the late 1940s his elder son Lloyd began hauling shavings during the day and delivering blackberries and pie cherries to the National Fruit Canning Co. in Seattle at night.

After high school graduation, Jim sold cars until 1958, when he joined his father and brother in the business of hauling wood shavings. By that time the cherry orchards had disappeared and they were out of the fruit business. They purchased a dump truck and hauled gravel and topsoil. In the 1960s they jumped into the aggregate business, and in 1966 they purchased 97 acres near the SIR Raceway in Kent.

Al Parker, Ron Scott, and Lloyd and Jim Iddings formed a partner-

ship, and in 1970 the partners, known as the Soos Company, bought 100 acres on Jenkins Creek in Covington. To help finance this transaction the Soos Company joined with Lakeside Industries. Lakeside bought out the 97 acres near the raceway, and the Soos Company retained ownership of the Covington property. In 1973 the Soos Company asked Lakeside Industries to purchase 20 percent of an additional 50 acres in Covington. In 1984 Jim Iddings bought out his brother's interest in the properties, and in 1989 he bought half of the 50 acres, known as the Carney property, from the Soos Company. This is now the site of Iddings Inc., run by Jim and his son James Randall. Begun in 1989, the company serves as a recycling center. Stumps are run through Northwest Wood Recyclers and Iddings Inc. sells the wood products to contractors. The property is one of two legal sites for dumping yard waste, which is also funneled through Northwest Wood Recyclers. Jim's company also offers a U-Haul service selling topsoil, gravel, and aggregates.

Today Iddings Inc. employs 27 people. Jim's son Randy heads the underground utilities end of the business.

"We have hauled a lot of Kent soil from the valley floor to the East Hill over the years," Jim says. "Coming from a farm family, it was hard to watch the rich soil along the valley floor covered with warehouses," he adds. Along with the industrial development, Jim has noticed other changes in the Kent area. "We used to know everyone," he adds with a smile. "Now you are lucky to pass a single car you recognize on the way to town."

Jim has been a long-standing member of the Kent Chamber of Commerce, and his company has sponsored Kent soccer teams and Little League baseball.

NORTHWEST METALS

ABOVE: During World War II Northwest Metals manufactured a number of products used by the military. Here, a press delivers a completely formed clip used for the M-1 Garand rifle.

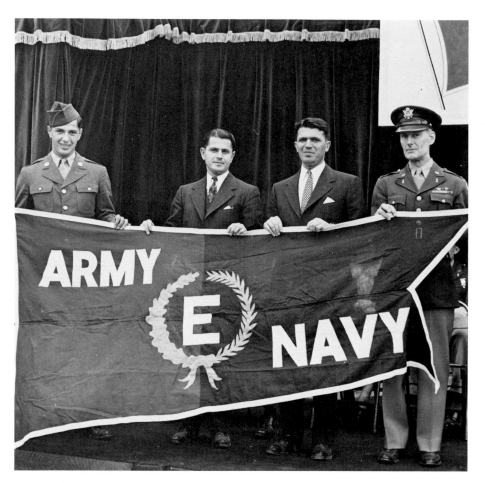

LEFT: The three Parker brothers (from left, Sam, Joe, and A.F. "Abe") and an unidentified officer proudly display the "E" Award flag to Northwest Metals for outstanding achievement in the war effort.

Northwest Metals was a family-owned business from its founding in 1921 until it was sold in 1964. Even after it was purchased by the William Wallace Company, Joe Parker continued on as part of the management team.

It all began when Frank Parker immigrated to the United States from Russia in the early 1920s. He began a small business making buckets, tubs, and garbage cans. Parker made the cans by hand in the morning and sold them in the afternoon. By 1921 he had started Northwest Metal Products in Seattle. With his new business underway and flourishing, he went back to Russia and returned to Seattle, bringing his family with him.

Parker died in the late 1920s and his sons—Joe, A.F. "Abe," and Sam—carried on the business. Joe was studying journalism at Columbia University at the time of his father's

death, and dropped out of school to take over the company. He assumed the role of president, his brother A.F. was vice president, and a few years later the youngest brother, Sam, joined the business.

The three brothers moved the company to Kent in 1936. Located on 8.89 acres at 401 North Fourth Avenue, Northwest Metals originally faced Sixth Avenue rather than Fourth Avenue.

According to an early historical account, Northwest Metals was one of the few factories in the country and the only one on the West Coast operating on a guaranteed plan for its employees. Factory workers were guaranteed at least 10.5 months' pay regardless of whether they worked three months or 12.

In its infancy, Northwest Metals manufactured one of the broadest

lines of metal products of any plant in the West. Specialty items included ski bindings and mailboxes. It was the only plant to manufacture rural mailboxes west of St. Louis.

In 1939 the company employed a crew ranging in size from 30 to 70 workers and had a payroll averaging $50,000 per year.

During the war years, the company expanded rapidly as the need for military equipment grew. It was during this time that Northwest Metals proudly flew the Army/Navy "E" Award Flag for its "outstanding achievement" in war production. Their major war assignment was the production of cartridge clips for the M-1 Garand rifle. Northwest Metals also produced antisubmarine net canister tanks for the U.S. Navy, prefabricated duct, building products and metalware for Army and Navy camps, stampings for overseas Army housing, shower-stall assemblies, and materials for federal and state housing projects.

After the war, under the management of the Parker brothers, Northwest Metals boasted more than

The company now produces 3,800 different items and employs 195 workers at their Kent headquarters.

one million dollars' worth of giant presses, shears, and other fabricating machines. It was gulping down 7,000 tons of steel annually to produce an endless supply of more than 100 different metal products. An aggressive sales force had pushed the company's sales volume from $3 million to $3.5 million in 1963.

In 1964 Northwest Metals attracted the attention of its major rival, and in May of that year the company was purchased by the William Wallace Company of Balmont, California.

Despite hopes of expansion and greater financial resources, the company did not fare well under the William Wallace management. Due to labor problems and a steady decline in sales, the company closed its doors in August 1968.

In October 1968 Noll Manufacturing, a California company, bought the company assets. Barry K. Miller was appointed general manager. It was not long before Miller established a network of wholesale distributing customers and a product line that includes many of the same products formerly produced by Northwest Metals. Garbage cans, buckets, tubs, mailboxes, and wheelbarrows, along with sheet-metal building products including rain gutters, down spouts, vents, and flashings are part of the product line. Heating products, including furnace pipe and fittings for air-conditioning and ventilation systems are large production items.

For Miller, moving to the Pacific Northwest was a dream come true.

He had visited the area as a youth and vowed he would one day return. When the opportunity of managing Northwest Metals was presented to him, he jumped at the opportunity and has never regretted his decision.

Miller also decided to rename the company its original name, Northwest Metal Products Co., with the abbreviation of Norwesco.

The company now produces 3,800 different items and employs 195 workers, a large force considering there were only eight employees when the company was rejuvenated in 1968.

Products manufactured at Northwest Metals are shipped to Alaska and Hawaii and are transported to Oregon, Washington, Idaho, Utah, Montana, Alaska, Hawaii, and British Columbia via a fleet of 15 tractors and 30 trailers.

In December 1986 the company purchased its major West Coast competitor, General Metalcraft in Portland. Within four months, all equipment and some employees were moved to the Kent location. The move added an additional 35 percent

to the company's overall production. Since 1980 Northwest Metals has purchased four companies.

In 1980 Dellmar D. Noack was made vice president/operations after working at the company for more than 30 years. Miller is now president of Noll Manufacturing, but he continues to oversee operations of Northwest Metals. In recent years, the 209,000-square-foot company has undergone a face-lift with the addition of plantings and the removal of an 80-foot smokestack. "We don't smell like overripe cabbage anymore," Miller says with a grin. In the late 1960s and early 1970s the Libby plant, a nearby neighbor, produced sauerkraut, and the plant's drain ran under the Northwest Metal warehouse. "It got pretty odoriferous around here before the Libby plant closed down," he adds.

Expansion continues to be a high-priority goal for the company. In December 1989 Norwesco purchased a 20-acre site near Fife, Washington, to provide room for future growth. "We are growing and getting better all the time," Miller says proudly.

FLOW INTERNATIONAL

When 18-month-old Jessica McClure fell into a deep well in Texas, there seemed little hope of getting her out alive. After almost three days of effort to drill through rock surrounding the well, a rescuer contacted Flow International Corporation in Kent. At midnight the company loaded an 18,000-pound ultrahigh-pressure drill on a Federal Express jet, and three hours after drilling began Jessica was pulled from the well in a dramatic rescue few people will forget.

The waterjet that saved Jessica's life was developed and manufactured at Flow International Corporation. It is a patented technology using an ultrahigh-pressure intensifier pump that pressurizes water up to 55,000 pounds per square inch and forces it through a nozzle as small as 0.004 inch in diameter, generating a high-velocity waterjet at speeds up to 3,000 feet per second. When abrasives are entrained into the waterjet, the high-velocity abrasivejet can cut virtually any material. Whether it is giving new life to the William Penn bronze statue standing above Philadelphia's City Hall, or removing deteriorated concrete from a highway bridge, Flow's waterjets will do the job.

As the leading manufacturer of ultrahigh-pressure waterjets for industrial cutting, drilling, and hydromilling, Flow has delivered more than 1,700 waterjet systems to a variety of industries in 45 countries. Waterjets are now used to clean paint-clogged surfaces; cut fiberglass insulation; slit and cross-cut candies, bread dough, and bakery goods; cut molded fiberglass helmets; and cut paper and tissue products.

The ultrahigh-pressure water jet was first developed by Flow Research Company, which became Flow Industries, a privately held company with a mission to develop new businesses based on advanced technologies. To develop the market for this technology in factory applications, the Flow Systems Division of Flow Industries was formed in 1974. By early 1983 the Flow Systems Division had sold approximately 300 Waterknife systems into 11 industries in 26 countries. The Flow Systems Division spun off as a separate public company in March 1983.

In February 1989 Flow Systems, Inc., acquired ADMAC, Inc., and expanded its application of waterjets to mining, construction, and industrial cleaning, in addition to automated factory waterjet cutting and drilling. ADMAC, Inc., produced hydromilling systems designed for concrete removal. The concrete removal rate of a FLOW hydromilling system is equiva-

The PASER II is a new abrasivejet cutting device with the capability to cut with a very high degree of accuracy for an entire 24-hour, three shift operation without adjustment or tool change.

lent to that of 15 jackhammers. The new company was named Flow International Corporation.

The company has begun to make greater in-depth market penetration overseas by expanding its capabilities in West Germany and Taiwan into full operations centers. Today, Flow International employs 344 people worldwide. Further market expansion came when the company developed standard slitting and cross-cutting systems for the paper, tissue, and fiberglass insulation material industries. They also developed standard X-Y shape-cutting systems for cutting heat-sensitive metals and hard-to-cut materials such as aluminum alloys, stainless steel, and titanium.

Through a distribution agreement Flow International will also sell and service gantry robotic waterjet systems worldwide. These systems are used in the automotive and aerospace industries. New technologies continue to contribute to expanded markets for Flow International. The PASER II is a new abrasivejet cutting device with the capability of cutting for an entire 24-hour, three-shift operation without adjustment or tool change, while maintaining an accuracy of 0.005 inch. A new pump and hose that has a burst pressure of 100,000 pounds per square inch (psi) allows Flow International to offer cost effective hydromilling services for the removal of deteriorated concrete from highway bridges, parking garages, and other concrete structures.

Future goals for Flow International include developing strategic partners in key markets worldwide and expanding waterjet systems and hydromilling services markets.

No other equipment can cut objects like candy bars cleaner and cheaper than the Flow Systems' Waterknife™.

FLOW RESEARCH, INC./QUEST INTEGRATED, INC.

It was out of Flow Research that the ultrahigh-pressure waterjet technology was developed into a product line for Flow International, FlowMole, and FlowDril. The research began in Dr. Y.H. Pao's basement in 1971 when he founded Flow Research, Inc., as a small research/engineering consulting firm. In May 1990 Flow Research, Inc., was renamed Quest Integrated, Inc. (QI^2), in recognition of the new and broad scope of research activities underway.

From Dr. Pao's basement, the fledgling Flow Research moved into Plemmons Industrial Park in Kent. There, Dr. Pao, Dr. John Olsen, and others began the research and development of the ultrahigh-pressure technology that subsequently served as the basis for the Flow family of manufacturing and service companies. In 1977 the company was moved to a new site among the cornfields and small farms then existing along the West Valley Highway.

Today, QI^2 is made up of three major technical divisions: Applied Physics Division (APD), Advanced Systems Division (ASD), and Technology Division (TD). The Applied Physics Division conducts research and development work in the areas of experimental and computational fluid mechanics, aerodynamics, solid mechanics, and ocean sciences. The APD staff includes several well-known scientists in the field of fluid dynamics, including coastal and ocean fluid dynamics. A number of QI^2 scientists have gone on to teach at academic institutions, including the University of Washington, Massachusetts Institute of Technology, the University of Maryland, and the University of Notre Dame. Computational modeling has been one of the major activities in the Applied Physics Division. QI^2 is the only small research business given the privilege of a direct link to the Cray-2 computer at the National Aerodynamics Simulator, a national supercomputational facility managed by NASA. The amount of time used by QI^2 on that computer was ranked third in the nation, following two of the NASA research centers.

The Advanced Systems Division solves problems in the areas of automatic systems, sensor technology, electro-optics, nondestructive evaluation, microprocessor- and computer-based controls, and analog and digital electronics. ASD also provides computer programming services. Systems have been developed to conduct such tasks as automatically gauging and inspecting parts at throughput rates of 1,500 parts per minute within tolerances to 0.0001 inch, straightness determination of hypervelocity test tracks, and rapid, real-time inspection of internal boiler tube surfaces with laser devices.

The Technology Division provides specialized engineering, design, and development services in the areas of high-pressure technology as well as liquid-jet and abrasive-waterjet cutting. Equipment has also been developed to improve mining, drilling, and excavation operations, as well as the decommissioning of nuclear facilities. One project involving TD's work with the Department of Energy's nuclear programs is the development of two advanced abrasive-waterjets for use in facilitating nuclear decontamination and decommissioning activities.

The original Flow Research, now Quest Integrated, building along West Valley Highway in 1978.

FLOWDRIL

In 1971, at the founding of Flow Industries, Inc., that company's founders foresaw the oil and gas drilling market as the largest single market application for ultrahigh-pressure jet cutting technology. There were only two problems: to pump 10 to 20 times the volume of fluid then possible with the early smaller ultrahigh-pressure pumps; and to deliver the pressurized fluid stream up to four miles downhole, under intense heat and pressure conditions, without leaks or loss of pressure.

By late 1985 Flow decided it was ready. The company sponsored an $11.9 million research and development partnership and launched FlowDril Corporation as a "spun-off" company from the Flow parent in 1985.

Prior to the FlowDril technology, the process of drilling for oil and gas involved setting a tri-cone rock bit with mechanical cutters on the bottom of the hole. The bit was then rotated to break up the rock. This process can become very expensive when working in harder rock formations due to the slower penetration rates and shorter bit life. The FlowDril system uses high-pressure fluid jets to slot and weaken the rock so that it is easier to break up with mechanical cutters. The FlowDril system's jet-assisted bits can drill up to five times faster than conventional bits.

Through fiscal year 1990, Flow-Dril has spent nearly $18 million on the development of the ultrahigh-pressure drilling system. The company has attracted the attention and the funding of several large institutional investors, including Grace Drilling Company, the largest U.S. drilling company. In joint venture with Grace, FlowDril is now commencing the commercial introduction of the system as a specialty drilling service. The first commercial system was delivered in February

An ultrahigh-pressure jet-assisted drill bit.

1990 and has already shown excellent results, achieving sustained increases in drilling speeds of up to three times conventional rates of penetration to almost 10,000 feet. Commercial revenues are expected to ramp up significantly when three additional FlowDril systems are delivered in late calendar year 1990, with accelerated deliveries thereafter.

John B. Cheung is president of FlowDril. He joined Flow Industries in 1974 and has served as president of FlowDril since 1987.

FLOWMOLE

There is an alternative to blocked driveways and devastated landscaping when the local utility company needs to replace the buried cable around your home. That alternative is the technology commercialized by FlowMole Corporation, "spun-off" from Flow Industries, Inc., in 1984. FlowMole, a six-year-old public company with $41 million in revenues, provides steerable, horizontal boring services to utilities in the United States, Canada, and eleven European countries.

The concept of using ultrahigh-pressure waterjet technology for underground utilities was begun in 1978, when the research arm of Flow Industries, Quest Integrated, Inc., contracted with the Electric Power Research Institute to develop novel methods for replacing failing underground electric cables. By 1983 the technology was sufficiently developed to warrant raising $10.4 million in a research and development partnership to complete a commercial prototype and launch FlowMole. Commercial operations commenced in 1985.

Since then the company has grown rapidly. In 1989 FlowMole installed 425 miles of cable in the United States, and revenues have increased steadily to $41 million in fiscal 1990. In recognition of the company's dramatic growth since 1984, *INC.* magazine named FlowMole to its 1989 "*INC.* 100" list of the fastest growing public companies.

John R. Potter is president and chief executive officer of FlowMole. He joined Flow Industries in 1983 and served as vice president and chief operations officer of FlowMole before becoming president in 1988.

FlowMole recently installed new telecommunication lines at Mount Vernon, George Washington's home on Virginia's Potomac River. The FlowMole trenchless technology preserved the site's pristine landscape.

CITY OF KENT

The thriving town of Kent, a settlement of 763 citizens, was bustling on the eve of its incorporation. The sound of the Puget Sound Shoreline Railroad whistle could be heard as it pulled into the town depot. Two general stores, a saloon, a drug store, a hotel, a post office, and a Methodist church formed the core of Kent, named after the leading hop-growing county of Kent, England.

Prior to incorporation the settlement had gone through sporadic name changes. James Henry Titus and Henry Yesler each purchased half of a large farm in the area where Kent is now located. For a time the western portion of the area became known as Yesler, and the eastern segment was known as Titusville. However, by 1888 the name of Kent was used by most people.

The county commissioners held a meeting in May 1890 to call an election for the authority to incorporate. The votes were cast in favor of incorporation.

Citizens also cast their ballots to elect the first officials of the incorporated town. Aaron T. Van de Vanter was declared mayor and C.F. Allen was elected the first clerk. Kent's first mayor was an enterprising hops farmer, real estate developer, and civic activist. He went on to serve as a senator in the Washington State Legislature and later ran successfully for King County sheriff.

Mayor Van de Vanter called the first regular meeting of Kent's newly elected town council in May 1890. The minutes of the first meeting have been lost, but the first ordinance established the time and place for meetings and stipulated that any city council members who missed a meeting without a valid excuse would be fined five dollars.

Council minutes and ordinances from early city council meetings provide insight into the problems and personalities of those forming Kent's

early city policies. Ordinance No. 8 prohibits lewd dress, abandonment of animals, saloons open on Sunday, houses of ill fame, driving a horse or mule over eight miles per hour, vandalism, resisting arrest, and not helping an officer when called upon.

Minutes from early council meetings show Van de Vanter to be somewhat of a penny pincher. He was highly concerned about the cost of running the city's electric light plant. He also suggested reducing

When the City of Kent celebrated its centennial on May 28, 1990, over 2,500 people came out to the Kent Millcreek Canyon Earthworks Park to share the birthday cake and join in the special festivities. The three-day celebration attracted over 45,000 participants into the city with fine restaurant booths, a beer garden, stage entertainment, and other feature events.

the salaries of the city employees, but ran into council opposition. By 1892 Kent had a well-established fire department. In 1898 the city budgeted $2,125 in expenses and had receipts of $2,870.

The first city hall was built on the corner of Second and Gowe streets, a few years after the town was founded. A new brick municipal building designed by Kent's city engineer, A.S. Leeper, was built in 1921 at the same location. The second city hall included city offices, a library, and a fire station. The present city hall, built at 220 Fourth Avenue, is an impressive four-story brick structure. It was designed by Fred Bassetti and dedicated on October 2, 1971.

Following World War II, Kent was ready for a change. Beginning with Dave Mooney, succeeding mayors accepted the challenge and carried on the vision of those who had served before them.

When Dave Mooney was elected mayor at 23 years old, he was the youngest mayor in the country. During his 10 years in office he organized the Kent Police Department under civil service and was instrumental in having the city become a part of the statewide retirement system. He worked tirelessly to promote the Kent parks and recreation program. During his tenure all the water mains in downtown Kent were replaced. New sources of water supplies were developed, and 3,900 acres were implemented with water service, sewer service, and roads.

When Alex Thornton was elected mayor in 1958, the town had grown from one square mile to 17 square miles and the population had increased from 2,500 to 17,000.

Under Thornton's leadership, new fire stations were acquired along with new trucks and more personnel. The police department was enlarged, fluoride was added to the water, and water and sewer lines were placed along East Valley Highway, which encouraged development of the East Valley industrial sector. Streets were improved and a new

Since 1909 there have been only three city clerks in Kent. They are Lake Erie Price, Brick Bridges, and the present clerk, Marie Jensen. City of Kent mayors are:

A.T. Van de Vanter 1890	W.H. Overlock 1917
J.W. Titus 1891	W.L. Fulp 1919
W.H. Overlock 1893	David Leppert 1921
J.J. Crow 1894	A.N. Berlin 1925
George Wood 1897	R.W. Murker 1927
B.A. Bowen 1901	S. Boucher 1931
W.H. Overlock 1907	R.E. Wooden 1935
M.M. Morrill 1909	Grant Dunbar 1943
I.P. Calhoun 1911	Dave Mooney 1947
E.W. Bereiter 1912	Alex Thornton 1958
M.R. Hardy 1914	Isabel Hogan 1969
W.J. Shinn 1916	Dan Kelleher 1985

utilities building was constructed.

A supporter of environmental issues, Isabel Hogan served 16 years as mayor. During her term trees were added on city streets. Parks and recreation facilities were expanded, including Mill Creek Canyon Earthworks Park and Russell Road Park. Kent Commons, an indoor recreation building, was constructed. The Saturday Market was developed and expanded to include fruits and vegetables, plants, and handmade arts and crafts. Also during Mayor Hogan's term, the Kent Arts Commission was established in 1972.

Under the leadership of the present city council and Mayor Dan Kelleher's administration, the City of Kent has been addressing the community's top priority issues. In the past four years, the Kent Highlands landfill has been closed, the new Kent Senior Activity Center has been opened, and Kent roads and streets have been significantly improved, including Smith Street, Reith Road, James Street, and West Valley Highway. Kent's downtown central business district has been enhanced with new art murals to identify the historic district and the completion of the Kent-Kherson Peace Park to honor

the new sister-city of Kherson in the Soviet Ukraine. In addition, the Riverbend Golf Complex with a new 18-hole golf course and clubhouse and the North Industrial Fire Station have been completed.

Today the City of Kent is proud of its many parks, its golf course, its colorful Saturday Market, and its multitude of year-round community events. Its recreational facilities offer a wide range of family activities. Community education programs such as the Drinking Driver Task Force help make Kent a safe place for families to live.

In the future, the City of Kent looks forward to completion of the public/private Centennial Center, a four-story office building with multi-level parking located across the street from city hall, completion of a new library, and expansion of the east-west traffic system. In addition to the remodeling of the downtown fire station and the opening of the police/fire training center on East Hill, new stations on West Hill and in Covington will provide increased public safety. The city also looks to a revitalization of the central business district by encouraging new economic development.

SEATTLE-TACOMA BOX CO.

Wooden signs nailed to a weathered post direct visitors to the Seattle-Tacoma Box Company in Kent. Once inside, walls covered with photographs and a decorative stack of wooden boxes and crates allude to a colorful history.

Despite two fires, two economic collapses, a drowning tragedy, high lumber prices, and stern competition from larger companies, this box-making dynasty has become one of the most successful family-owned businesses in the region.

Washington's governor, Booth Gardner, recently set aside October 23, 1989, as "Nist Family Day" to commemorate the family's 100 years of accomplishment and contribution to the economy of the state.

It was the great Seattle Fire that sparked Jacob Nist to build the first box-making company. Nist, born in Kentucky, moved his family to the Seattle area in 1880 and worked in Seattle's thriving lumber industry. When his place of employment was destroyed by the Seattle fire of 1889, he and his son Michael opened the Queen City Manufacturing Company at the corner of Westlake and Thomas near Denny Way. They made a variety of wood products including sashes, door frames, and egg crates, but by 1905 boxes were the company's main product. That year the company name was changed to the Seattle Box Co. Bursting with

Queen City Manufacturing Company—predecessor to Seattle Tacoma Box.

business, the company outgrew its quarters and moved to what is now the corner of Spokane Street and Fourth Avenue South.

Seattle Box was the only building in the area, and it was almost completely surrounded by water. It was accessible only by horse team and railroad trestle. Today the area has been filled with dredgings from the Duwamish River and is now Seattle's major industrial district.

Michael, who had taken over the reins of management in 1905, stepped down in 1917. Two of Michael's 17 children, sons Ferdinand and Joseph, became the new leaders of the company.

In 1922 Seattle Box bought Tacoma's Calef Box Company and renamed it the Tacoma Box Company. The Tacoma operation was kept separate from Seattle Box until 1975, when the two operations were merged and

George Lang leans on a 1910 truck used by Seattle Tacoma Box Co.

became Seattle-Tacoma Box Co. A new plant was built in Kent to accommodate the new, larger facility. The fourth generation of Nists—Emmet, Gene, and Ferd—is now in charge of the family business.

The Depression years were difficult. Gene Nist, who is now vice president of the company, remembers the grim days when he managed the Tacoma operation. During that time production was reduced to two or three days a week. Beginning as a hand nailer at 12, Gene has worked for the company for 53 years. During

Seattle Tacoma Box's Nist family team: (front left to right) Mike, Rob, Ferd, Gene, and (back) Emmet.

those years he has taken Tacoma Box from seven employees in 1938 to a high of 47 during World War II, converted the plant to electric power in 1944, and led the way to finding innovative postwar markets during the 1950s. He also developed corrugated technology and later opened a booming business in Hawaii.

Perseverance and hard work have served the company well over the years. "Back in the early days we worked 18-hour days," says Emmett Nist, the 74-year-old president of the company. Emmett warms up when he starts talking about the more than 100 employees who produce $20 million in sales annually. "We operate as a family and our employees stick around until they retire," adds the president, who has been with the company for 51 years.

Ferd, the youngest Nist brother running the company, has worked there for 32 years. The 51-year-old serves as "point man" of an expanding enterprise. Ferd joined Gene in developing products to sell in Japan, Hong Kong, Singapore, Hawaii, and Alaska.

The fifth generation of Nists is coming along in the company tradition of innovation and hard work. The company was computerized in 1975, and with its sophisticated, automated production of wood boxes, tubular packages, bed frames, and other products, providing a broad and reliable product base, Seattle-Tacoma Box Co. promises to serve its market. That is why it is still around after 100 years.

VALLEY STORES

Today, motor homes stand ready for the customers of Valley I-5.

Hard work, dedication to service, and adherence to the golden rule have helped make the Valley Stores, Valley I-5 in Kent and Valley Pontiac-Buick-GMC, Inc., in Auburn, two of the most successful vehicle dealerships in the state. Their success has been recognized by a steady increase in sales, tremendous growth, and special recognition from the auto and RV industry.

In 1989 Ron Claudon was selected Washington State's Auto Dealer of the Year. In 1988 Valley Pontiac-Buick-GMC, Inc., was chosen by *Time* magazine as one of the top 17 new car dealerships in the nation. Valley I-5 in Kent has been honored through the years as one of the largest, most successful motor home dealers in the nation. In 1966 the Valley Stores purchased four of the first ten Winnebago motor homes built; in 1986 Frank Lee, Valley's president, was presented the keys to the 200,000th Winnebago motor home built.

Owners Frank Lee, Ron Claudon, and Floyd Miller have seen the company grow from eight employees and one million dollars in vehicle sales in 1961 to the present 132 employees and more than $55 million in annual sales. The team joined forces at Valley Garage, Inc., located at the corner of West Valley and Meeker in Kent. After two years Valley Garage of Auburn was formed, selling GMC trucks only. Pontiac and Buick lines were added and the store name became Valley Pontiac-Buick-GMC, Inc. Claudon is president of the Auburn store and Frank Lee is president of Valley I-5 (Valley Garage, Inc.) in Kent and chairman of the board for the combined operation.

While Lee has been a driving force on the management end of the business, Claudon has reached out to the community. To honor his community involvement, he was recently voted one of Auburn's 10 most outstanding leaders. Among his many community achievements, he has served as director of the Auburn Chamber of Commerce, serves as fire district commissioner, is a trustee of Green River Community College, and was president of the Washington State Auto Dealer's Association.

Although the Valley Stores are not a family-owned business, there are a number of family members in the business. Lee's brother Jerry Reese is General Manager of Valley I-5; Ron's brother Dennis Claudon is the general sales manager. Lee's son and daughter are also employees of the company. Claudon's son is operations manager at Valley in Auburn, and the list goes on.

Many of their employees have been with them for more than 20 years. The customer and employee care can easily be seen at the Valley Stores. One can depend on professional assistance and the best of care in all departments at either Valley location. The Valley Stores are a total transportation headquarters, with Pontiacs, Buicks, GMC trucks, boats, and motor homes, all available at a dealership locally owned since 1918.

Valley Garage was opened in 1918 by Roy McHugo and is owned and managed by Frank Lee, Ron Claudon, and Floyd Miller.

METEOR COMMUNICATIONS CORPORATION

Five men did more than wish upon a star when they began their meteor communications company in 1975. Capitalizing on the concept of using the fiery trail of meteors, more commonly known as shooting stars, to reflect radio signals from one point of earth to another, these enterprising engineers began their business in a small, three-bedroom house. From this humble beginning the Meteor Communications Corporation now generates more than $10 million in yearly sales and resides in a contemporary 50,000-square-foot, two-story building in Kent.

It all started when Ray Leader, Dale Smith, Tom Donich, Bob Dickerson, and Don Sytsma began working together at the Boeing Company on the research and development of a technique that uses the natural phenomenon of meteor bursts rather than manufactured satellites to transmit messages. When Boeing terminated its work on meteor-burst activity, they decided to go out on

The five original founders of Meteor Communications: (left to right) Don Sytsma, Bobby Dickerson, Ray Leader, Dale Smith, and Tom Donich.

their own and develop a product line using meteor-burst communications.

Dale Smith's home was used as company headquarters. With bedrooms for offices and a kitchen for a laboratory, they provided engineering service for the design and installation of the meteor-burst system.

Angela Swanson was their first employee. She had been cleaning house for Smith while she attended Kentridge High School, but she was soon promoted to typist and later secretary. Swanson is still with Meteor Communications and is completing her degree in marketing at the University of Washington.

In 1977 the company moved from the Smith home to Plemmons Industrial Park in Kent. A big break came in 1979 when the fledgling company had an opportunity to bid on a large government request for the Department of Energy. It was a $7 million project and promised unlimited opportunities for the small company. Everyone worked around the clock to complete the proposal. Swanson joined forces, typing well into the night despite her own busy schedule as a contestant in the Miss Kent Pageant. Sytsma recalls Swanson, dressed in her evening gown, intently typing the proposal an hour before she was to compete in the pageant.

The proposal was accepted, much to everyone's excitement, but the final contract was not scheduled for signing until early December 1979. A series of complications and the holidays delayed the signing. Two days before the contract was to be finalized, Department of Energy funds were cut and the contract was never signed.

"We were all terribly disappointed, and we thought about shutting down, but we decided to hang on," Sytsma says.

During this time, they concentrated their energies on a project known as Snotel, an acronym for SNOwpack TELemetry. Designed for the Department of Agriculture's Soil Conservation Service, Snotel is a network of non-staffed monitoring stations designed to measure snow accumulation. Snow measurements made continuously in high mountain valleys, most of them inaccessible by road, help scientists predict spring flooding, irrigation prospects, and erosion. Meteor Communications has now installed 600 stations.

When Mount Saint Helens erupted in 1980 the Department of

Don Sytsma, president of MCC, with a 6520 Master Station.

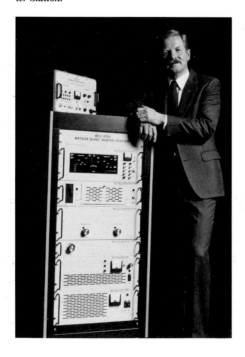

The Kent corporate headquarters of Meteor Communications.

Agriculture needed a remote station and communication system to monitor future eruptions. Meteor Communications was asked to design a product to fill that need. With the completion of that product, the consulting firm became a full-service company capable of designing, engineering, and installing meteor-burst products.

In 1983 the company moved from Plemmons to 72nd Avenue on the West Valley Highway. Over a three-year period from 1983 to 1986, they expanded from a 5,000-square-foot building to 35,000 square feet, employed more than 100 people, and were spread out in three buildings.

To bring the enterprise under one roof, the company entered into a joint venture with First Western Development and formed Meteor Building Associates to purchase seven acres and build their present headquarters, a two-story building at 6020 South 190th Street in Kent.

The building was completed in July 1986, and in September of that year Meteor Communications was purchased by the Titan Corporation, based in La Jolla, California. At the time of the sale, the company had recorded sales of $10 million and grew to $15 million by the end of the year.

Unfortunately things did not work out as anticipated, and Titan's promises of marketing and financial support were not forthcoming. Combined with the recession and fewer government contracts, sales dropped to $8 million and employees were cut to 85 people. In May 1989 management purchased Meteor Communications Corporation and formed an employee-owned company.

With the constant demand for meteor-burst systems developed by the company, production and sales are on the upturn. The firm remains the world leader in meteor-burst communication. At present the U.S. Air Force is using meteor-burst communications along with satellite communication for transmitting radar data that monitors Alaskan air space. As satellite communications are interrupted, meteor-burst equipment takes over. Meteor systems in Argentina monitor snowpack levels in the Andes. In China Meteor Communications records the level of rivers feeding into hydroelectric systems. In Europe acid rain is monitored along with the water quality of the Thames River in England. Meteor communication devices have been planted along the Chinese/Soviet Union border to send short encoded messages back to Beijing. Other systems in Australia, Canada, Indonesia, Egypt, and Europe have been set up to monitor solar radiation, tides, water supplies, motorway fog, and snow conditions.

Most recently Meteor Communications has been found to be applicable to mobile communications systems in vehicles. With Meteor Communications radios on trucks, dispatchers will know where trucks are at all times.

The five founders have remained active in the company until recently, when Leader and Dickerson retired. Sytsma is president of Meteor Communications Corporation, Donich serves as vice president of engineering, and Smith is manager of Test Engineering.

A remote Meteor Communications site in picturesque Ushuaia on the southern tip of Argentina.

MILES SAND AND GRAVEL

The Miles family has been in the sand and gravel business since 1938. Frank Miles' grandfather came to Auburn in 1943 to produce sand and gravel for the Rainier Ordnance Depot, a military project.

Operating out of his home, the elder Frank Miles began supplying sand and gravel for projects all over the West Coast, including the Roza Dam, Bluett Pass Highway, and the Grant County Airport.

In 1943 he purchased 18 acres at 1201 "M" Street in Auburn and, with his son Walt, began expanding the business that today boasts 17 sand and gravel sites, 150 trucks, and 300 employees.

Walt's son Frank was not planning to go to work for his father. He had a teaching career in mind, but when his father became ill and died at the age of 56, young Miles went to work at the sand and gravel company. A civil engineering graduate, he was running the business at age 25.

In 1969 Frank purchased a sand and gravel site in Kent at 8240 South 228th and expanded acreage at the Auburn site. The company now owns 140 acres in Auburn.

From the beginning, Miles Sand

and Gravel has been community oriented. Before swimming accidents posed an overwhelming insurance liability, the company encouraged civic groups to use their acreage and lake for picnics and soccer games. The company has donated material and equipment to various public and Eagle Scout projects. The Kent plant was a winner of a Kent City Beautification Award for attractive landscaping.

Employees helped during the frequent floods that covered Kent before the Howard A. Hanson Dam was built in 1963. Frank remembers loading sandbags on and off trucks to stem overflowing water.

The early 1970s marked the beginning of Miles Sand and Gravel expansion. In 1973 Frank bought Kenyon Materials in Bremerton. The company now has plants in Port Orchard, Bremerton, Silverdale, and Belfair in Kitsap County. Concrete NorWest was his next acquisition. Continuing to expand gravel sites, he purchased Ross Sand and Gravel in 1981 to service the fast-growing Snohomish County area. Next came two plants in Tacoma, and in 1988 he purchased Cascade Ready Mix in Burlington. In 1989 Cascade Materials in Shelton was added to the list of acquisitions.

From 1982 to 1986 Frank owned a ready-mix operation in An-

A 1967 model Miles Sand and Gravel truck.

chorage, Alaska. "That was an amazing experience," Frank says, recalling the economic oil boom and the excitement it generated.

Miles Sand and Gravel has enticed Frank's children into the business. Now his daughter, Lisa Kittilsby, and his son, Walt Miles, are following in their father's footsteps. Like their father, Walt and Lisa worked summers at the Auburn and Kent plants. They each graduated from Pacific Lutheran University and are active in the management of the company. Lisa returned to the sand and gravel company for three years and then headed back to school with her husband for their master's degrees in finance. Her husband, Tim, is a CPA and "a whiz with computers," Frank says proudly. Tim has joined the family business as a financial accountant.

Sound management and steady growth have resulted in the company's acquisition of 2,000 acres of land throughout western Washington. More than 4 million tons of washed aggregate and crushed rock is produced per year at these sites.

"We have seen tremendous growth in our company and in the areas we serve," Miles says. "Our goal is to keep up the pace with the steady growth of the area and to meet the ever-increasing demand."

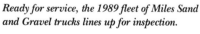

Ready for service, the 1989 fleet of Miles Sand and Gravel trucks lines up for inspection.

RALEIGH BICYCLE

Known for its production of air and space transportation, Kent has come down to earth with the addition of the Raleigh Bicycle Company. The 100-year-old Raleigh Company opened a 65,000-square-foot facility in Kent in May 1985. With the help of 120 employees, the company makes 100,000 bicycles each year and earns $50 million in total sales.

It all started back in 1887 when Frank Bowden, a successful attorney and avid cyclist, recognized the value of bicycles and purchased a small

Ron Weed uses state-of-the-art technology to build a Technium® U.S.A. bicycle at Raleigh's new $10 million, 65,000-square-foot manufacturing facility in Kent.

bicycle workshop on Raleigh Street in Nottingham, England. The Raleigh Shop developed a "safety bicycle," the first bicycle with a chain drive to the front wheel. Bowden was convinced that there was a potentially enormous market for this innovative bicycle.

Bowden very quickly expanded the Raleigh Company to a five-story factory and brought out a wide range of models to appeal to every sector of the bicycle market. The business

was boosted even further when 23 innovative designs were introduced by Raleigh at the Stanley Cycle Show in 1890.

During World War II Raleigh developed a new design for paratrooper use—the folding bicycle. After the war the company expanded its business worldwide and continued its innovations with a new rim that would accommodate both caliper and pull-up brakes, bright new colors, metallic finishes, and track racing bicycles.

Raleigh introduced lightweight bicycles to America in 1933. The American bicycle at the time was a cumbersome, unwieldy affair weighing more than 60 pounds with wide wheels. The sleek new Raleighs were an immediate success.

When Raleigh decided to sponsor the 1983 U.S. Cycling Team with advanced aerodynamic bicycles, a new process of thermally bonding dissimilar materials was developed. The Technium® process also helped Raleigh develop a high-quality bonded-aluminum bicycle at affordable prices. The Raleigh Company in Kent is dedicated to producing many bicycles using the new Technium® process.

In 1982 Huffy Corporation purchased the license to manufacture and distribute Raleigh bicycles in the United States. Many factors went into the selection of Kent as one of Huffy's bicycle facilities. Community support for the bicycle industry was a major consideration, along with a large per-

For the committed sport touring rider, the Technium® U.S.A. Olympian combines the revolutionary Technium® frame with all-alloy, high performance componentry and a tighter frame geometry for greater speed and power.

centage of the population committed to outdoor sports. King County's active support of the Rails to Trails program, a plan to convert old railway tracks to bike trails, was also a factor. With so many bicycles to be shipped worldwide, Kent's close proximity to air and shipping facilities and railroads also attracted the bicycle industry.

In 1988 Huffy sold back its licensing agreement to Raleigh. In the meantime Raleigh was purchased by Derby International S.A. The U.S. portion of Raleigh is controlled by the Derby Cycle Corporation, a subsidiary of Derby International. Dan Downing is vice-president/operations at the Raleigh Company, and Chuck Wilke is president of the Derby Cycle Corporation. The Kent company produces a number of bicycle brands for other Derby Corporation divisions, including Nishiki, Cycle Pro, and Haro.

With the advent of the mountain bicycle, featuring sturdier wheels and frame, many older people have taken up cycling, according to Downing. In 1989 mountain bikes comprised 65 percent of the company's total sales. But Raleigh officials predict that the lightweight bike of the past will come back in the near future.

SHANNON AND ASSOCIATES

Rivaling the Pied Piper's faithful following, Bob Shannon's integrity, hard work, and amiable manner have contributed to a lifetime of loyal clients for Shannon and Associates, the largest certified public accounting firm in Kent. The harmonica-playing CPA is known far and wide for his service to clients and his love of music.

Shannon and Associates had its beginnings in 1956, when Bob Shannon opened a small CPA office at 318 West Meeker. Before coming to Kent, Shannon graduated from the University of Washington and worked for the accounting firm of Ernst and Ernst in 1946-1947. During World War II he was a Navy pilot and later served as a commanding officer of the VI 891 Fighter Squadron. After the war he worked as a comptroller for Sunset

Electric, and in 1953 he opened his own CPA office in Seattle, before moving to Kent three years later.

During the early years of his practice in Kent, he rented office space from Don Bell, owner of Don Bell Insurance, and he recalls talking to clients over the sound of Don Bell, Sr., playing the organ. "He had one finger missing, but that didn't slow him down a bit," Shannon says with a grin.

Wading through knee-deep water when Kent flooded several times per year is another memory Shannon has of the years when he was establishing his CPA firm. At the time he had one employee, but was busy serving a steadily growing clientele.

During this time the young CPA taught accounting classes as an associate lecturer at the University of Washington. He also served as Commander in the U.S. Naval Reserve.

In 1963 Shannon built the 603 Building at 603 West Gowe. Then, like today, Shannon worked endless hours to solve his clients' accounting problems. "He has so many loyal clients because he always has been willing to accommodate people," says Mary Ann Burns, a partner in the firm. "They know if they come to him with a special problem, he will do whatever it

Shannon and Associates is the largest and longest-standing CPA firm in Kent.

takes to solve it," she adds.

Along with building his business, Shannon also participated in community activities. He served as president of the Seattle Industrial Kiwanis Club and has been a member of the organization for 38 years. Recognizing the need for housing to accommodate executives moving into the community, Shannon played an instrumental part in establishing Meridian Valley Country Club, a community of upper middle-class homes. He served as club president in 1969.

Shannon expanded his firm again in 1975 when he purchased the 604 Building. Specializing in corporate taxation for closely held companies, the firm grew to include eight employees. In 1978 he sold the 603 Building, and on January 1, 1979, he sold the 604 Building and acquired the 606 Building on West Gowe in Kent.

Shannon merged with other accounting firms until 1981, when he formed the present partnership with Dick Lackey and Joe Poff. Mary Ann Burns joined the partnership in 1983. In 1986 he sold the 606 Building to his partners. He continues to practice and serve loyal clients, but he is taking time to pursue his study of music, a lifetime love.

Shannon and Associates is the largest and longest-standing CPA firm in the Valley. The firm serves clients from the greater Puget Sound area as well as Alaska, Oregon, and California. The staff of 25 includes 19 accountants, who offer a diversity of expertise and a wide range of services, including accounting and auditing, taxes, retirement plans, and business and management consulting. The firm was recently ranked among the Puget Sound's Top 25 Certified Public Accounting firms in the *Puget Sound Business Journal.* Shannon and Associates continues to grow with the closely held companies it serves as a partner in business.

BURDIC FEED INC.

Burdic Feed has been in business for 100 years and has been a mainstay in Kent for 35 years. The feed store remained in the Burdic family for three generations, until 1980, when it was purchased by Bernell Guthmiller, owner of Signal Electric Co., his brother, Laverne (now deceased), and father Herbert Sullivan (now deceased).

Coming from a farm family in South Dakota, Bernell Guthmiller was intrigued with a farm-related business. Since taking over ownership of the 60,000-square-foot enterprise, Guthmiller employs 40 and turns out 2,400 tons of grain and 50,000 pounds of dog food per month. Other products available include horse and bird feed, pets and pet supplies, tack, grain used in slug bait, and a large supply of farm and garden tools. Cages of rabbits, kittens, and birds greet the steady stream of customers coming into the store.

Burdic Feed began as a general store in 1889. In 1901 Guilford Burdic and his son Ray sold the general store and opened a retail feed store in South Park, an area in southern Seattle. Using mule-drawn carts, the store owners delivered feed to nearby farms. Soon the streetcar line opened to South Park and residential development grew. When the Duwamish River was straightened, changing the geography of South Park, Ray Burdic moved several blocks to 14th Avenue South.

Chester "Chet" Burdic, Ray's son, graduated from the University of Washington in 1933 and opened another retail feed store on Highway 99, known then as Duwamish Junction. In 1935 he moved his operation to Ross Marginal Way. He built a small mill and manufactured his own feed. When his father died, Chester bought out his father's interests and bought additional retail feed stores.

Early in 1941 Chet was called into the service and was given one week to find a manager for his four stores. He called on one of his fishing partners, a former manager of the Sperry Flour Co. in Seattle, to take over.

When he returned from military duty in 1946, Chester built a larger mill on rail at the East Marginal store location and closed two of the less profitable retail stores. Many of his customers were moving as Seattle's growing population pushed small farmers farther south. To preserve closer contacts with his customers, Chester moved the Burdic Feed Mill to Railroad and Smith Street in Kent in 1954 with three employees. By 1980 the feed store employed more than 30 people and supplied farmers with fertilizer, feed, and garden tools and supplies.

Then, after 20 years of Guilford Burdic's ownership, 30 years of Ray

---

RIGHT: R.F. Burdic's second store in Seattle as it was in 1891.

BELOW: This Burdic Feed mill at Smith and Railroad streets supplies Kent area farmers with fertilizer, feed, garden tools, and provisions.

Burdic's ownership, and 47 years of Chester Burdic's ownership, Burdic Feed was sold to Signal Electric Co.

The new owner has found a ready market for feed store supplies, including a number of dairy farms along with a growing population of horses. Last year Burdic Feed grossed $7.5 million.

In recent years, two new feed stores have been added, including one in Tacoma and one in Monroe, Washington. In the future, Guthmiller hopes to expand Burdic Feed Inc. to cities and towns throughout western Washington.

HOWARD MANUFACTURING CO.

Not only have three generations of Howards climbed ladders of success, but they have built them as well. More than one million ladders of all sizes and shapes, from the 24-inch stool to the 44-foot extension, have been produced by the Howard family since the turn of the century.

Charles J. Howard began the business in Washington as a broom maker like his father, who owned a broom-making company in Indiana. In 1901 Charles opened the Washington Broom Works at a small site in Belltown, Seattle. After making a move to Rainier Avenue, he restructured his broom company to include the production of butter molds, pastry boards, and washboards. The company, renamed the Washington Broom and Woodenware Co., flourished until 1917, when the broom department was sold and the remaining interest reorganized under the name of Howard Manufacturing Co.

Charles continued as president until his death in 1919. His wife, Alice, stepped in and, with the help of a manager, operated the successful firm. In 1928 the company moved to Kent, enticed by the nominal price offered by the city for a plant formerly owned by Western Rubber. The site,

located at 421 Sixth Avenue North, included two large buildings on several acres. The offices used by Howard Manufacturing are part of the original structure.

The eldest son, Paul, assumed direction of the company in the 1930s and was later joined by his brother William.

Before the war the company established an assembly plant in Brooklyn, New York, where products made in Kent were assembled. During World War II a shortage of lumber forced closure of the New York assembly plant. Washboards were eliminated in 1945. At one time, Howard Manufacturing was the second-largest producer of washboards in the country.

To combat increasing rail costs, an assembly plant was established in Los Angeles in 1947. That plant burned to the ground in 1958, but it was continued in another location.

In 1962 Paul Howard began producing the Ventwood Panel, made of wood rails doweled together that range in length from two to 16 feet. Although originally designed for decks, the product has been used for decorative wood ceilings, screens, benches, tables, and shelves. Ventwood can be found worldwide, including airport ceilings in New Mexico and Hawaii. The capitol ro-

Following in his father's footsteps, Charles J. Howard opened this broom-making company in 1901 in Belltown, Seattle.

tunda in Micronesia and the King Hussein War College in Jordan use the attractive paneling made in Kent. The paneling has been sold for use in Bermuda, South America, Mexico, Canada, and all over the United States.

Along with the company's production of wood ladders, Howard Manufacturing now produces fiberglass and aluminum ladders. More than 42 models of up to 20 different sizes for a total of 255 standard stock Howard ladders are manufactured at the Kent plant. Since the late 1970s and early 1980s, fiberglass steps and extension ladders of all sizes have been machine-produced. Using its advanced mechanized system, the company's 100 employees turn out thousands of ladders each year for distribution in 11 western states.

Howard Manufacturing is now spread over 100,000 square feet on nine acres. Along with an assembly plant in Los Angeles, the company has warehouses in San Francisco, Salt Lake City, Denver, and Phoenix.

Since 1976 Paul's son Chuck Howard has been president of the company and his brother Jim is vice president in charge of sales. John Howard, a cousin, is comptroller, and Bill's other son Phil Howard is involved in Howard ladder sales. Bill and Paul Howard remain on the company's board of directors.

Howard Manufacturing moved to Kent in 1928.

ERLING LARSEN AIR CARRIER INTERIORS

Erling Larsen employee Shirley J. Tozer at work on weather covers used to protect cargo containers.

Erling Larsen's courage to forge ahead despite obstacles that might have stopped others has led to the success of his business, Air Carrier Interiors. During the growing years of the company that he has personally expanded and developed, his firm manufactured a great variety of products for Boeing and Heath Tecna, among others.

His company has grown from a one-man, part-time operation in 1960 to a well-established company of 30 employees.

Air Carrier Interiors was founded in 1958 by Charles Redmon, Keith Petrich, and Robert Carrier. Located in a Quonset hut on Boeing Field, the small business provided custom interiors for light aircraft.

Larsen, who had worked for Charles Redmon since the age of 14, began working at the newly organized company part-time while he attended classes at the University of Washington.

Bob Carrier was bought out in 1959, and for a year the upholstery shop was dormant. In 1960 Redmon offered Larsen 25 percent of the business at no cost if he would take over the company. Larsen dove in and began learning everything he could about the upholstery business, including sewing the upholstery on a Fairchild 24 airplane. For the next two years, the company took custom jobs, mostly for light aircraft.

In 1962 Larsen had the idea of selling engine cooling shrouds for Bell Helicopters to the U.S. Army. Before signing the contract, he had to be sure the bank would underwrite the cost. "The value of my business was less than the amount of the contract," Larsen remembers.

In 1967 Larsen bought out his partner, Redmon, and contracted with Heath Tecna Air Cargo Division to manufacture all of its nets and weather covers used to cover cargo containers.

The Heath Tecna contract was Larsen's initiation into manufacturing and scheduling work loads to meet contract demands. The manufacturing schedule meant the creation of two night shifts and the addition of five new employees.

In 1967 Larsen's wife, Ila, joined her husband, helping out as secretary and bookkeeper for the rapidly growing company. She continues to work for Air Carrier Interiors on a part-time basis.

During the 1970s Larsen expanded his business to Alaska as Air Carrier Interiors became the repair source for the covers and cargo retainers on Wien and Alaska Airlines. He also began developing products with Boeing. The baggage restraint nets produced for Boeing have continued to be a mainstay for Air Carrier Interiors today.

As manufacturing began to take the place of custom work, employees became more permanent and the company grew steadily.

In 1979 the company was bursting its seams at the Boeing Field location and moved from its original 5,000-square-foot area into an 18,000-square-foot facility north of Kent at 22645 76th Avenue South. At the time, the area was surrounded with bushes and a pond. Now it is filled with office buildings, warehouses, and fast-paced traffic.

Larsen expanded into the industrial market and hired Bill Null as his tarp production manager. Null had been in the canvas protective-cover materials business and brought his customer base with him.

Larsen has a pay-as-you-go philosophy. "I haven't borrowed money since the mid-70s," Larsen adds with pride. "We don't take on any venture that is beyond our capability."

In his few free hours, Larsen spends time with his family and works with high school youth programs. He serves as district commissioner for the Boy Scouts and has been a member of the Kiwanis Club for 21 years.

(Left to right) Andrew G. Fanning, shop foreman; Erling M. Larsen, president; and Michael J. Moore, general manager.

BOEING AEROSPACE & ELECTRONICS

In 1960, when President John F. Kennedy announced that the U.S. would launch a mission to the moon by the end of the decade, the impact was felt nationwide. In the Pacific Northwest, nowhere was that impact more deeply felt than in Kent, Washington, where more than 10,000 people were employed at the Boeing Space Center on space-related projects.

Prior to that time, the Boeing Company was involved in the space industry, but it was Kennedy's impetus that led Boeing to consolidate its efforts into one large division, now known as Boeing Aerospace & Electronics.

Since its opening in 1964, the Kent facility has produced the Lunar Orbiter spacecraft which were built to select a landing site on the moon, the first stage of the Saturn V rockets that sent astronauts on their way to the lunar surface, and the wire-wheel moon buggy that carried them around when they landed. Continuing its commitment to space programs, the company designed and builds the Inertial Upper Stage (IUS), which boosts payloads into higher orbit. Today Boeing Aerospace & Electronics employs more than 25,000 people nationwide.

The Boeing-built E-6 serves as a Navy communications aircraft.

George H. Stoner, former vice president of the space division, was a prime mover in the establishment of the huge Boeing facility in Kent. More than 550,000 yards of fill material was brought in to prepare the 320-acre site in the Kent Valley. In the beginning two large buildings were constructed. One, a long low structure of 100,000 square feet, was built to house microelectronics and the materials and processes laboratories. The other large building, including an 85-foot-high bay area, housed the space flight environment and flight simulation research laboratories.

The space flight simulation laboratory was designed to train astronauts to operate spacecraft before they were sent on space missions. Equipment was set up for simulating rendezvous inspections and docking in orbit. Later the flight simulation laboratory was doubled in size to help pilots practice aerial refueling.

The space environmental lab housed 11 vacuum chambers ranging from one cubic foot to a giant 50-cubic-foot chamber capable of containing any spacecraft on the drawing boards. Space vehicle models and material specimens were tested in the extreme conditions of outer space.

When NASA needed to choose a landing site on the moon, Boeing developed the Lunar Orbiter. The spacecraft was capable of photo-

The Inertial Upper Stage (IUS) boosts space shuttle payloads into a higher orbit. This photograph shows the IUS as it is deployed from the shuttle's cargo bay.

graphing craters the size of a manhole cover. While working on the Lunar Orbiter, Boeing also began developing the first stage of the Saturn V rockets, preceding the Apollo 11 flight carrying men to the moon on July 20, 1969. After the Saturn V, Boeing built the moon buggy that carried astronauts over the lunar surface. Three moon buggies remain on the moon.

In the early 1970s the U.S. space program lost momentum because no major follow-on projects had been approved or initiated. For a time it looked as though the space program might fall apart completely. Scrambling to find work for Boeing engineers, George Stoner headed a task force to look into new projects. One was a contract with the Department of Energy to build a controlled personal rapid transit system to alleviate clogged highways. A fully automated system was designed to carry 21 passengers per car and travel 30 miles per hour. A working prototype of the Boeing "people mover" was set up on the Boeing Space Center site where employees tried out the vehicle. The people mover was put in

operation in Morgantown, West Virginia, and Japan.

Other Space Center projects during this period of diversification included water purification, asphalt plants, and wind-powered energy systems. When NASA decided to move its rocket testing facilities to another part of the country, Boeing turned its attention to agriculture. The company turned the former desert testing site into productive farmland, proving the feasibility of farming the land.

Diversification activities led Boeing into several major programs with a variety of customers. Instead of NASA as its sole customer, Boeing became involved in defense projects for the U.S. government and foreign countries.

Along with the IUS, the most sophisticated unmanned spacecraft in the United States, Boeing scientists and engineers designed and built some of the most important parts for the Hubble Space Telescope. The company provided the metering truss which holds the telescope's optical mirrors in alignment during launch and in the harsh environment of space. Boeing also designed and built the focal plane structures that help Hubble view the universe with exciting new clarity.

Another Aerospace & Electronics project is Boeing's Airborne Warn-

Boeing's Kent facility produced the familiar Lunar Orbiter spacecraft as well as the astronaut's wire-wheeled surface-roving vehicle.

ing and Control System (AWACS), the world's most advanced airborne early warning system. It is a survivable surveillance, command-and-control platform that enables all-altitude surveillance of targets over land and water.

For the U.S. Navy, Boeing is producing the E-6A, a survivable communications system that will provide vital emergency communications between national command authorities and the U.S. Navy's ballistic missile submarine force.

Boeing also is involved in efforts to improve U.S. defense capabilities. These include modernizing Minuteman missile forces, and the Rail Garrison concept, which calls for Peacekeeper missiles to be based

aboard railroad trains. The Hard Mobile Launcher was designed to transport small intercontinental ballistic missiles. The Short Range Attack Missile (SRAM) II air-to-ground missile is carried aboard the B-1 bomber.

The Boeing Aerospace & Electronics division also designs and manufactures substantial quantities of electronics for all Boeing divisions and receives about 200 research and development contracts each year. The division manages a substantial portion of Boeing's internal research budget.

The Boeing Aerospace & Electronics division continues to grow and diversify, perennially contributing to King County's dynamic economic strength.

A bird's-eye view of the Boeing Space Center in Kent.

Patrons

The following individuals, companies, and organizations have made a valuable commitment to the quality of this publication. Windsor Publications and the Kent Chamber of Commerce gratefully acknowledge their participation in *Kent: Valley of Opportunity*.

Amway Regional Distribution Center
Boeing Aerospace & Electronics*
Bowen Scarff Ford-Volvo, Inc.*
Burdic Feed Inc.*
City Beverages Distributors, Inc.*
City of Kent*

Curran, Kleweno and Johnson*
FlowDril*
Flow International*
FlowMole*
Flow Research, Inc./Quest Integrated, Inc.*
Heath Tecna*
Howard Manufacturing Co.*
Iddings Inc.*
Erling Larsen Air Carrier Interiors*
Meteor Communications Corporation*
Miles Sand and Gravel*
Northwest Metals*

Poe Construction, Inc.*
Pozzi Bros. Transportation Inc.*
Raleigh Bicycle*
Seattle-Tacoma Box Co.*
Shannon and Associates*
Union Pacific Realty Company*
Valley Daily News*
Valley Stores*

*Partners in Progress of *Kent: Valley of Opportunity*. The histories of these companies and organizations appear in Chapter Eight, beginning on page 89.

Bibliography

Given below is a selected listing of general references consulted throughout the book, followed by references especially helpful within individual chapters.

GENERAL

Bagley, Clarence B. *History of King County, Washington.* Vols. I-IV. Chicago & Seattle: S.J. Clarke Publishing Co., 1929.

Cameron, C.E. *Kent, Washington: USA Northwest Heritage.* Seattle: Ballard Printing & Publishing, 1978.

Flewelling, Stan. *Farmlands. The Story of Thomas, A Small Agricultural Community in King County, Washington.* Auburn: Erick Sanders Historical Society, 1990.

Green River Community College, History Department. "Kent, 1910-1960." Oral History Project Tapes.

Hanford, Hon. Cornelius H., ed. *Seattle and Environs 1852-1924.* Vol I. Chicago & Seattle: Pioneer Historical Publishing Co., 1924.

Pigott, H. C., ed. *History & Progress of King County, Washington.* Seattle: Charles J. Hutchinson, 1916.

Van Nest, Linda. "Kent, Washington—A Historic Overview." Kent: Kent School District, Curriculum & Instruction Division, 1989.

A Volume of Memoirs and Genealogy of Representative Citizens of the City of Seattle and County of King, Washington. New York: Lewis Publishing Co., 1903.

DIRECTORIES

Choir's Pioneer Directory of the City of Seattle and King County; History, Business Directory and Immigrants Guide to and throughout Washington Territory and Vicinity. Pottsville, Pa.: 1878.

Oregon, Washington and Idaho Gazetteer and Business Directory. Portland: R.L. Polk & Co., 1884-1885; 1889-1890; 1891-1892; 1901-1902.

Puget Sound Directory. Portland: R. L. Polk & Co., 1887, 1889.

Seattle City Directory. Vol. I. Seattle: R. L. Polk & Co., 1889.

Tacoma-Seattle Interurban Directory. Vol. II. Seattle: R.L. Polk & Co., 1909.

NEWSPAPERS

Daily Pacific Tribune
Kent Advertiser-Journal
Kent News-Journal
The Seattle Times
The Seattle Weekly
Valley Daily News
Washington Standard
White River Journal

CHAPTER 1:
The Lure of White River

Buerge, David. "Requiem for a River." *The Weekly* October 16-22, 1985.

————. "The King County Wars." *The Weekly* February 8-14, 1984.

Dalan, Hunt, and Wilke For Geo Recon International. "Cultural Resource Overview and Reconnaissance: Green River Flood Damage Reduction Study." Report to Dept.

of the Army, Seattle District Corps of Engineers. Seattle, 1981.

Denny, Arthur A. *Pioneer Days on Puget Sound.* Seattle: The Alice Harriman Co., 1906.

Lane, Barbara. "Political and Economic Aspects of Indian-White Culture Contact." Vol. I, "Summary of Anthropological Report in U.S. vs. Washington." Vol. VIII, "Identity and Treaty Status of the Muckleshoot Indians." Vol. IX, "Anthropological Report on the Traditional Fisheries of the Muckleshoot Indians." Unpublished materials. November 1972.

Noel, Patricia. *Muckleshoot Indian History.* Auburn: Auburn School District No. 408, 1980.

Waterman, T. T. "Puget Sound Geography." National Anthropological Archives, Manuscript No. 1864, circa 1920.

CHAPTER 2:
The Fertile Valley

King County Department of Public Works. *King County Road Book No. 4.* (For Plats).

Meeker, Ezra. *Hop Culture in the United States.* Puyallup: E. Meeker & Co., 1883.

Owens, John. *Thomas Moody Alvord, Pioneer Merchant, Trader, Boatman, Farmer of Pialschie, Washington Territory.* Auburn: White River Valley Historical Society, 1984.

Pence, William Ross. "The White River Valley of Washington." Master's thesis, University of Washington, Seattle, 1946.

CHAPTER 3:
Forging a Community
"Description of White River Valley Country." *The West Shore* October 1877, 17.
"Hop Fields of Puyallup and White River Valley." *The West Shore* Vol. 10, November 11, 1884, 345.
Kent Town Council Minutes: 1893-1899.
Kent Town Ordinances: 1890-1899.

CHAPTER 4:
Progressive Times
The Coast March 1902, p. 60.
—————, July 1905, p. 28.
—————, April 1907, p. 264.
—————, June 1909, p. 382.
King County Road Engineer. "Fifth Annual Report of the County Road Engineer - 1939 - State Golden Jubilee."
Marshall, James. *The Carnation Company History.* 1939.
Nishinoiri, John Isao. "Japanese Farms in Washington." Master's thesis, University of Washington, Seattle, 1926.
Swett, Ira, ed. *The Puget Sound Electric Railway.* Los Angeles: Interurbans Electric Railway Publications, July 1960.
Roberts, W. J. (Chief Engineer). "Report on Inter-County River Improvement on White-Stuck and Puyallup Rivers in King and Pierce Counties, Washington." January 1920.

CHAPTER 5:
Harvesting the Gifts of the Land
Abel, Don (WPA State Administrar). "Report on Community Progress." Seattle, 1937.
Kent Commercial Club. "Kent, Washington" (Promotional brochure). Circa 1925.
Ito, Kazuo *Issei: A History of Japanese Immigrants in North America.* Translated by Shinchiro Nakamura and Jean S. Gerard. Seattle: Japanese Community Service, 1973.
Norikone, Koji, ed. *A Pictorial Album of the History of the Japanese of the White River Valley.* Auburn, Wa.: Japanese American Citizens League, 1986.

CHAPTER 6:
Changes in the Wind
Hanson, Howard A. "More Land for Industry." *Pacific Northwest Quarterly* January 1957.
King County Department of Planning and Community Development. "A River of Green. Recreation and Conservation on the Upper and Lower Green River." Report for the Green River Basin Program, 1978.
King County Planning Commission. "Duwamish Valley Study Area Renton-Kent-Auburn." Seattle, 1957.
—————. "Studies for a Comprehensive Plan." Vol. 8, Kent Report. February 1953.
Rainboth, Edith Dyer, and Bayard O. Wheeler. "A Survey of the Housing, Income, Population of Kent, Washington and its Environs." Bureau of Business Research, College of Business Administration, University of Washington, Seattle, 1949.

CHAPTER 7:
The Valley Transformed
City of Kent. "Kent Parks and Recreation Plan—1982."
—————. "Report of the Human Services Study Committee on Human Services Policies." August 1986.
Jordan, Cal & Associates. "The Kent CBD: An Economic Analysis." Report for Kent Planning Department. April 1975.
Kent Chamber of Commerce. *1989-1990 Membership Directory and Community Profile.*
Kent Planning Commission. "Kent Comprehensive Plan." Adopted January 3, 1977, by Kent City Council.
Kent Planning Department. "Agricultural Lands Study." June 1982.

Index

Photo Identification
Special Collections Division, University of
Washington Libraries:

Page 8: #NA 3985
Page 10: #NA 3994
Page 11: #NA 249
Page 14 (bottom photo): #UW 8497
Page 30: #NA 663